Errata

P. 26, par. 3, L. 10: It should read "See Note 8" (not Note 1)

P. 26, par. 5, L. 2: expression (not exposing)

P. 29, L. 4: proto-Christian (not pro-Christian)

P. 44, Note 17, second line from bottom: mystical (not mythical)

P. 52, par. 1, last line: ca. 106 (not 102)

The
JESUS
IDEA

The
JESUS
IDEA

Arnold M. Rothstein

Prometheus Books

59 John Glenn Drive
Buffalo, NewYork 14228-2197

Published 1993 by Prometheus Books

97 96 95 94 93   5 4 3 2 1

Library of Congress Cataloging-in-Publication Data

Rothstein, Arnold M.
    The Jesus idea / by Arnold M. Rothstein.
       p.   cm.
    Includes bibliographical references.
    ISBN 978-0-87975-862-2
    1. Jesus Christ—Person and offices. 2. Salvation—History of doctrines.
I. Title.
BT250.R685   1993
232′.8—dc20
                                                93-39806
                                                CIP

To Adrian, who taught me that the insights of a child reveal a degree of self-understanding not often attained by adults.

Contents

Preface

And of more than these, my son, beware: of making many books there is no end . . .

—Ecclesiastes 12:12

The effort of writing a book such as *The Jesus Idea* over a period of eight years calls for some justification, particularly when there are so many on the general subject as to be exhaustive. Most books in the scholarly genre tend toward textual or philologic analysis or an aspect of these, while in the popular species, one finds fancy, romance, or novella. What is unique about the topic itself is the unavailability of "new" evidence nor, in the case of a shadowy figure, can there be any. A new book on this subject is, necessarily, a "different" way of viewing old materials.

A dominant feature of most books is their agreement on point of departure, on what is considered bald fact: the existence of a historical figure endowed with the title-name Jesus, historicity being established by indirect argument, not evidence in the empirical sense. For, how could the doctrine of Christianity exist and spread throughout the world without the actual substance of a real person? That "self-evident" fact is held as a prepossession, resting on the continuity of an institution that has claimed the support of millions of adherents for centuries: the affirmation of an idea is, itself, evidence of existence. This obvious datum is identified as constituting the very proof of an historical life that was lived. Moreover, if a Redeemer had the capability of rising from the throes of death, it is not possible, nor thinkable, that a life had *not* been lived. The circularity of the position and its *ad hoc* nature are patent, if one dares to raise the point of question-begging. Undergirding the a priori prepossession is

11

the tacit acceptance of gospel writings as historiographic record; thus is forged an impermeable compound, the ultimate key to a theography.

The present work is bold enough to aver that the requirement for *some* demonstration (beyond self-confirmation) has been gainsaid. Not only is there *no* recognition that a claim—never substantiated—has been advanced, there is also rejection at the very outset that a bald fact *requires* substantiation. For, one need not substantiate an abiding truth; its ongoing existence is sufficient verification. This book is, essentially, one of counter-argument against such a mode of reasoning and against prepossession offered as evidence.

The author disclaims special preeminence in the absorption of hermeneutical rules of exegesis, but he is comforted by the thought that in pursuing the lure of beguiling curiosity for more than a quarter-century, he has been led into darkened alleyways and the remote byways of pertinent literature and specialized subject matter. These have pointed to the realization that the mastery of all subdisciplines connected with the subject is beyond what one individual can achieve within a lifetime. Yet, there surely is a claim to the *utilization* of knowledge (to use Alfred North Whitehead's immortal phrase), not its mere archival assembling. In fact, the collection of knowledge, like the gathering of sea shells, can be of no productive consequence if clarity of vision is obscured by sheer volume. Thus, what is affirmed is the attitude toward, and competence in, handling the "glowing coals" of learning and scholarship with care and responsibility. "Warm yourself by the fire of the wise but beware of their glowing coals lest you be burned" (Ethics of the Fathers 2:15). Indeed, the warning may be interpreted literally!

One of the unfortunate features of much scholarly writing is that it is addressed primarily "in house," i.e., scholars talking to each other, with "drip-down" and diffusion often taking centuries. Then, too, scholarly work tends to severe self-limitation, i.e., making available original material without further comment, the diagnostic task being left to others, because the technician's effort of preparation and presentation has been so all-consuming. For instance, in the Letter of (apostolic father) Ignatius to the Trallians, IX.1, one reads: "Be deaf, therefore, when anyone speaks to you apart from Jesus Christ who . . . was truly persecuted under Pontius Pilate. . . ."[1] The term *under,* rather than *by,* utters volumes, but there are few, if any, exegetical comments on its significance as Christian theodicy. This work is, then, for the most part, a study in the interstices of selected writings—the author serving as theorist and expositor—aimed at a didactic and instructional objective. It is intended primarily as a reader for an educated and critical audience devoted to truth-seeking.

The plan of the author involved the presentation of discrete units of scholarship connected to a theoretical frame: how a Redeemer idea became historicized. Now, it is observed that most works of scholarly style, e.g., the spuriousness of the Christ passage in Josephus, are not even heard of, much less studied, by a wide audience, however intelligent, for several reasons. The subtle and often minute detail necessary for careful distinction demands requisite background of protracted exploration and reflection. Perhaps even more compelling is the competing allure of a good story over critical investigation and exposition. It may be that Oscar Wilde was correct in his observation that human beings cannot bear too much of reality. Thus, Nikos Kazantzakis's *He Who Must Die* or Martin Scorsese's *The Last Temptation of Christ* pique the fancy of the viewer, but it may be noted that such presentations are built upon the presumption of a fact of history. In this work, that presumption yields to an alternate explanation of etiological reconstruction—one that is not built upon modes and styles of thought of the first three centuries.

There must be thousands among the educated and discerning who want a simpler condensation of scholarship than highly technical studies, for whom an exploration of the etiology of the Jesus idea suggests more than ritualized acquiescence of a mythological framework. While the book is addressed to such a readership and strives to be nontechnical, it does not shy away from the abstruse in an attempt to be superficially popular. At the same time, there is recognition that preoccupation with the minute will necessarily restrict breadth of scope, it being paradoxical that decades of study are required to escape from the coils of single-track specialization. It is highly recommended that scriptural incidents and references within the text be reviewed in order to frame an appropriate context for the interpretive comments presented. In addition, explanatory material in the notes section of each part is intended to clarify, elucidate, and elaborate on the text.

Attention is called to some of the usages contained herein which depart from those typically employed in works on the subject area. Less are they the product of idiosyncrasy than they are the natural accompaniment to a work that explores the Jesus idea as the personification of salvation.

The title of the book posed a difficult problem, Jesus as a name being already a theological conclusion, as are Jesus *the* Christ or Christ Jesus. Initially, it was planned to refer to Jesus, not as a name, but as a title, *The* Jesus. Since that was rejected as creating unusual problems in style of expression, there is, instead, reference to *a* Jesus; in most cases it is accompanied by the Hebrew term *yeshua* to convey the idea that the name is the result of an hypostatization of the concept of salvation (*yeshua*).

Jesus *of* Nazareth, an existential assertion as well as a geographical claim, has also been rejected as historiographic conclusion. Jesus the Nazirite has been employed as a compromise substitute. (See chapter 3 on the origins of Nazareth.)

There are some widespread usages that have embedded within them hidden arguments or built-in conclusions. Unless compelled by stylistic concerns, they have been studiously avoided or explicated:

(1) New Testament–Old Testament is indicative of a larger theory of supersession, the one testament or covenant not merely replacing the other, but suggesting that the old was merely an introduction to the new.

(2) B.C. and A.D. are, of course, explicit theological arguments. The common era (C.E.) and before the common era (B.C.E.) are employed as preferable usages.

(3) The designation *Lord* was used differently two thousand years ago than is understood today. In Greek thought, *kyrios* meant "master," as did the Hebrew *adōn* or the Aramaic *Ribbōn*. (Acts 2:36: "God made Jesus both Lord and Messiah [*Christos Kurios*]"). Today, *Lord* is considered equivalent to God and is often so employed; in addition, it is believed to be an adequate translation of the Hebrew symbols YHVH (or YHWH). The translation/substitution is, however, not adequate, hence the letters YHVH are preferred as conveying the idea of the nontranslatable nature of the symbols.

In order to indicate pronunciation, there are orthographic alterations of titles and names, similar to the procedure known as *itacism*. Thus, Kenaan is preferred over the anglicized Canaan (Kaynan), the latter distorting Semitic pronunciation beyond recognition, as does Rabbi (long *i*), hence Rabee. Similarly the letter *Y* serves in the place of the *J* as in Yeriho for Jericho; other alterations—Metsada (Masada), Doketism (Docetism)—follow the preference for *less* distortion of an original sound, rather than reinforcing tonal-phonetic accretions imported from outside.

The application of the name "Christian" to describe group membership prior to the second century represents unwarranted anachronization. There were only messianists or christ-ists (descriptive terms rather than actual group names) who were represented by a variety of names such as Nazarenes or Natzoreans, Galilaeans, Ebionites, and others, which were to disappear later.

As will be evident, gospel writings are viewed not as historiographic records, but as creative devotional literature, i.e., liturgical expressions of conviction representing the objectification and concretization of an idea-form. Regrettably they function historiographically, willy-nilly, in the minds of many who may not even have much direct familiarity with them. Until the period of the Enlightenment, they have been represented as historiographic accounts of a single existence, a model to be admired, the ascription of historicity being necessary to a reexperiencing of the central events of the "life." The search within gospel writings for an historical person is a search for the embedding or renewing of faith (including martyrdom). Without it, there would hardly be a community of faith.

The expression, *The Gospel According to* Mark, Matthew, Luke, John (rather than, for example, Mark 14), is intended to suggest that the work represents a school, church, or collective or corporate entity, not the effort of a single author. (However, sometimes stylistic considerations will compel the less cumbersome, such as Luke 7, over *The Gospel According to. . . .)* In general, the use of individual names, particularly in biblical writings— even when clearly eponymous—results in misconstrual of historical movements through involuntary and reflexive conceptual retrojections. An eponym is one whose name serves as summary of an institution (place or people); the eponymous reference is to a collectivity, not a solitary individual.

On a final note, the book is not for those who, in advance, know all they need to know by listening to an inner voice repeat familiar thoughts and sayings. It is for those who are uneasy about unresolved questions left over from a distant Sunday school exposure.

Note

1. *The Apostolic Fathers,* vol. 1, trans. Kirsopp Lake (Cambridge: Harvard University Press, 1952), p. 221.

Introduction

For more than two millennia, an idea has been promulgated concerning the earthly manifestation of an actual aspect of divinity. The nature of the evidence presented for the divine manifestation has been entirely self-confirming and self-reassuring, essentially an ad hoc appeal to a huge group of followers who accepted it. An unassailable conviction, the idea was an outgrowth of a very human desire to mitigate the permanence of death as absolute extinction. To what extent are humans capable of ascribing substance to an idea which is nonsubstance? The answer is that hypostatization (as it is called) is a very distinctive human trait, to be found in everyday discourse, e.g., "time flies." Name changes or even alterations in spelling are often considered to be transformations of reality, or objects held in thought or uttered in spoken word become identified with the object itself; this occurs in the mention of tabu terms associated with vulgarity. In Soviet Russia of the 1920s, in order to usher in Marx's dream of a "classless society," hotel and train personnel were prohibited from referring to first *class* and second *class,* even though the actuality of the distinctions was maintained. Indeed, the history of the *process* of hypostatization and its near-relative iconization is a long and unusual one, a "manifestation" occurring in all anthropomorphic expressions and thoughts and, of course, in the stories of God-men.

The author realizes that he is dealing with popular belief, a subject receiving continuous and ongoing confirmation and approbation and which, through institutionalization into the social fabric for centuries, has long been absorbed into the current of individual thought and activity so as to be taken as reality itself. Nevertheless, the elements of that thought structure bears reexamination insofar as it is an attempt to apprehend what is also considered a mystery, a human translation of what pur-

17

ports to be a divine story. This book examines the attempt at such a translation as the personification of the Jesus idea.

Jesus is an idea of salvation substantialized and historicized over a considerable time span. The personification process of salvation constitutes a reweaving of material already in existence in literary forms (personalities such as Elijah in the Old Testament) and in the cultic practices of secret confraternities. Concerning the actual earthly existence of such an individual, we can know next to nothing, all efforts to recover a human history ending in failure. He exists purely as a portrait of supreme innocence and purity, a composite of traditions dating back to a proto-divinity representing the expression "*Yah* is salvation" ("*Yah* Saves").

The theory of salvation (or *yeshua*) represents a syncretism of ideas and dreams optimistically embraced by humans in response to the wretchedness and misery experienced in life, even the state of humanity itself being viewed by some as wretched. *Yeshua*—the Hebraic concept of which the Greek name Jesus is a translation—involved a recurrent hope among humans that "all things can be made anew." That hope provided the thematic material for the sketching of a portrait, an attempt to express what was essentially symbolic: triumph over death. The idea of *yeshua* had regenerative quality and made its appearance in a variety of forms over centuries. The theory of salvation gradually became personified and fixed within a singular individual, a composite of many savior-types, into whom life was breathed. The final outlines of that life (and death) were a construction of devotional and liturgical literature known as gospels, which were essentially declarations of conviction and theological summaries. In these liturgies, the salvation theory was historicized and personified as individual savior.

Most books in the subject area—especially those entitled *Life of Jesus*—employ conjecture and speculation, not as mere filler but as basic stock. Historicity is usually established by presupposition, the title itself, *Life,* already gainsaying the major question, or indirect argument is employed, neither being what we usually understand by the term "evidence" or "verification." Some conjectures and speculations are more plausible than others, that is, less free-floating, but it is the paucity of verifiable material that encourages a reliance on the imaginative. Even though what is asserted without grounds can simply be denied without grounds, it is believed that the analysis in this work offers an inferential structure for mooring and anchorage sufficient to resist the pull of high winds.

1

A Message from on High
The Conquest of Death

The Kingdom of God

History is *not* a chronicle of human events in Judaean conceptions of the second precentury and the first century of the common era. Rather, it is a sequence of events ordered by God; hence, the idea of historical evidence as we know it is foreign to it. Divine entry into ordinary events in the world alters or shapes the transpiring events themselves; consequently, they have no life independent of that cosmic intervention. "Evidence" appropriate to this fully enclosed conception is *conviction* and is equated with virtue. To affirm or confess the idea is itself to provide evidence. To say that Jesus was The Christ required no investigation of oral accounts of his life and death typical of police activity. It was sufficient and indeed meritorius to affirm the theory of divine intervention into the lives of mortals. Thus, the humanity of Jesus is taken as a certainty; it is the way God made himself manifest or immanent (within the world). A differing theological conception is that God is far-removed or transcendent (above worldly concerns), but that is not as comforting or reassuring. With this certainty, we know that God understands the human condition, since he deigns to become part of it.

This kind of historiography, better termed theography, is a narrative written by God himself. The only human contribution to it is recognition that it is a story of the coming Kingdom: "The Kingdom of God is at hand," and humans are able to participate in his coronation by bearing witness. The style of this succinct annunciatory formula, "the Kingdom of God is at Hand," is termed *apocalyptic*, that is, having to do with

19

revelation: insight coming from a divine source. The reported author of the formula, John the Baptist (Yo-ḥanan), was, according to accounts, a Judaean desert recluse who lived an austere life of meditation and of self-denial, and who was given to frequent ablution or bathing to rid himself of the hardening accumulations of iniquity. His message was simple and clear: "Repent" or turn away from the obvious evils of this world in order to cleanse oneself, to prepare a vessel fit to receive the blessings of God. That message was often heard in Israel, for example, in 600 B.C.E., in Jeremiah (Yirmi-yahu) 35:15: "Return now everyone from his evil way and amend your doings."

Although associations, brotherhoods, and confraternities reached back into a much earlier period, the message attracted followers and persisted over centuries. These associations or collegia were departures from the parent body of dominant ritual practice and distinguishable from it. Sometimes, such associations suffered ostracism because of their cultic differences from the mainstream; at other times, they were merely looked upon as anachronistic curiosities and oddities, and condescendingly tolerated much as the late twentieth century tolerates the Amish. There were also periods of legal disability and persecution by a zealous and strong central authority that saw in such voluntary associations a centrifugal force. At such periods, voluntary associations tended to coalesce and amalgamate. However, there was also attrition and falling away due to a loss of membership and loss of ideological fervor as a result of the inroads of progress, such as highways and technological advance.

Among the earliest groups in ancient Israel were such as necromancers, sun-worshipping cults, and fertility sects, to assure plentiful harvests through imitative magic. Such groups were actively suppressed by strong Yahuist monarchs (YHVH was the symbol of the official God); others persisted and through syncretistic reinterpretation of their cult practices were absorbed by another group. Two early Yahu-centered brotherhoods, particularly zealous in vow and practice, Nazirites and Rechabites (Nezirim and Rekhavim) seemed to have a history of more than a millennium and reappear a thousand years later under different names such as Nazarenes and Essenes. To which association John the Baptist (Yo-ḥanan) adhered, cannot be determined with any certainty, but his counterpart among the Rechabites (Rekhavim) of 850 years earlier (see Jeremiah [Yirmi-yahu] 35) may be recognized. Yo-nadav or Yeho-nadav, son of the sect's founder, Rekhav, is similar in meaning to the name Yo-ḥanan: the grace or gift of Yō. (Yō is a shorter form of Vahō or Yahu, the unpronounceable concept of the God of Israel.) That the Rechabites (Rekhavim) resembled the Nazirites (Nazirenes) in their vows of abstinence (from wine among other things) seems certain, and both brotherhoods bore traceable similarities to a confraternity called Nazarenes, which were later absorbed into the larger association of Christ-ists.

One or more of these collegia were bearers of a tradition of salvation (*yeshua*) coming from the outside, i.e., divine intervention. Indeed, the early history of Israel is saturated with the idea that its political aspirations were achieved not through autonomous military power but through God's overt actions. Such groups transmitted John the Baptist's (Yo-ḥanan's) theme of the Kingdom of God and tried to hasten it by proclamation: *Mara Na Tha,* Lord, Please Come!, which is the Aramaic invocation in *The First Letter of Paul to the Corinthians* 16:22; this in turn can be seen as an adaptation of the Hebrew Kaddish formula. One may recognize in the Lord's Prayer overtones of the Kaddish: "Hallowed be your name. Your Kingdom Come." In the Hebrew liturgy the doxology, a paean of praise to God known as the Kaddish, dates back to the first century C.E.; its crystallization is roughly contemporaneous with Paul's evangelizing, which gives us some insight into the thought(s) of the day.[1]

When the tradition of salvation (*yeshua*) by divine intervention began to be recorded and appeared in the writings known as the New Testament, a major characteristic becomes apparent: It is theography, *not* history. If the faith system of Christ-ology is purged of its historical features, what remains? Christ *is* as his interpreters present him. Apologists "demonstrated" the truth of Christ-ology not by contemporary evidence, but by textual casuistry; references were made to the Psalms and prophetic writings, which transformed the "Old" Testament into a prologue of the "New." To achieve this transformation, the interpreters relied on symbolism, allegory, allusion, and theosophy; more will be said of these later.

What is most arresting about New Testament material is that it is so radically different from most histories. The internal material of the New Testament reveals no evolutionary development of a people, as is the case with most national histories. Instead, a finished product is presented, as if the theography were autobiographical. *Sinlessness is personified and given substance.* It is this feature that is *new* in the New Testament. Certainly it differs from the Old Testament in message and style. In contrast, the "Old" does tell of the evolution and development of a people, but *that* story in Christological hermeneutics is largely wicked and sinful, and is seen as mere preparation for the fulfillment and full flower of the personification of *sinlessness* as a substantive being. In similar manner, all other divine savior-types are hermeneutically viewed as preparing the way for the true Divine Savior.[2]

Theography, then, in the first-century context, involved finding an oracular scriptural source in the Old Testament and linking it to an hermeneutical or interpretive outlook. Some know this device as homily or *midrash,* which involves sketching in a background scene and inventing dialogue, all with a moral or theological purpose. An example of a creative background scene plus dialogue is found in the narrative concerning thirty pieces of silver as the price of a betrayal ("the price set on a man's head"). Matthew 26:14–16 reads:

> Then one of the Twelve . . . went to the chief priests and said, "What will you give me to betray him to you?" They weighed him out thirty silver pieces. From that moment he began to look for an opportunity to betray him.

Then one reads in Matthew 27:5:

> So he threw the money down in the temple and left. . . . The chief priests took up the money . . . they used it to buy the Potter's Field, as a burial place for foreigners.

In Zechariah 11:12–13 one finds:

> I said to them, "if it suits you, give me my wages; otherwise keep them." Then they weighed out my wages, thirty silver pieces. The Lord said to me, "Throw it into the Treasury." [The Hebrew word *yōtzer* means "Potter," in Syriac, "Treasury."] I took the thirty pieces of silver—the princely sum at which I was paid off by them!—and threw them into the house of the Lord, into the treasury.[3]

The *silver* and *potter* occur in a different spatial context and at a considerable temporal distance, yet the phraseology is preserved to embellish a betrayal narrative and, in the words of Matthew 27:9: ". . . in this way fulfillment was given to the saying of the prophet Jeremiah . . . [sic]."

This kind of casuistic method, conceived as the human expression of theography, constituted truth and objective reality. It was built upon a basic conviction that could not be doubted any more than one's own existence could be doubted: Death has been conquered because salvation (*yeshua*), invested with a human body, rose from death. This was theography: the message from on high.

The very triumph of the socio-political movement to become known as Christianity was a conditioning of the thought process itself: It compelled attributing to the idea of salvation (*yeshua*) both personhood and superhuman nature. While the lowly personhood in its expressed actuality of a poor untutored preacher ended in utter failure and ignominy, within a century the name and claim of *yeshua,* the embodiment of salvation, spread throughout the Roman Empire, fired by a vision and an epistemological belief taken as axiomatic.

Divine Knowledge: A Gift Bestowed Upon the Chosen

The First Letter of John 2:22 declares: "Anyone who denies that Jesus is the Christ is nothing but a Liar." Not only is this a definition of Truth, but it reveals an epistemological method as well of securing truth: "You will know the truth and the truth will set you free" (*The Gospel According to John* 8:32). That knowledge is a divine gift bestowed upon the chosen, as is forcefully stated in *The Letter of Paul to the Galatians* 1:1: "From Paul, an apostle commissioned not by any human authority or human act, but by Jesus Christ and God the Father who raised him from the dead," and further in Galatians 1:11-12: "I must make it clear to you, my friends, that the gospel you heard me preach is not of human origin. I did not take it over from anyone; no one taught it me; I received it through a revelation of Jesus Christ."

Paul proclaims a theory of knowing that cannot be assailed, since it is not of human origin. Although—unlike other apostles—he had no personal encounter with Jesus (Yeshua) while he walked the earth in human form, he does claim apostolic appointment on the basis of singular revelation. Indeed, in Galatians 1:22, Paul refers to difficulties with some of his coreligionists who may have questioned his recently discovered zeal as a missionary of a new faith community. However, he insists on his claim to apostolic status on the basis of a theophanous vision of Jesus, as he traveled the road to Damascus on a mission of rooting out heresy (Acts of the Apostles 9:1-6). In that revelation, he is transformed from "Saul, why are you persecuting me?" to Paul the "servant of Christ Jesus."

While revelation as expressed in the theophany between Paul and his Master would not be admissible as evidence in a twentieth-century Western court because of the impossibility of public corroboration, one has to think in first-century terms. This means that revelation is the *preferred* epistemological system above any other; mere human knowledge is looked on with disdain.

Today we speak of inspiration or special gifts such as those contributing to the inventions of Michelangelo, Bach, Mozart, Beethoven, Frank Lloyd Wright, Shakespeare, or other artists of equivalent magnificence and magnitude. The concept of inspiration or special gifts—however elusive—is usually comprehended as creative force or energy. However, in the five hundred years from the third century B.C.E. until the third century C.E., the language of "Thus Saith the Lord . . .," "the mouth of the

Lord has spoken it," ". . . that the Scriptures might be fulfilled" would be comprehended at once as truth itself, an incontestable epistemological asseveration.

Julian Huxley employs another modality:

> The desires and aspirations of the mind conspire with its organizing faculties . . . to organize vital experience on a new level, above that of the ordinary self, above that of all merely discursive activity, in which new intensity is gained through so much more than usual being seen and felt together in a single organized moment of spiritual perception.[4]

This apparently equates the experience of revelational insight as organizing activity of the mind; it is a description that might explain a twentieth-century attitude toward "spiritual perception" occurring in a twentieth-century context, but it is not a certainty whether the same explanation would be applied to the first century. Even if Rudolf Bultmann is correct in his observation that "Modern men take it for granted that the course of nature and history like their own inner and practical life is nowhere interrupted [or perforated] by the intervention of supernatural powers,"[5] even that deemed inspirational, somehow first-century revelation is viewed by the same twentieth-century individual as sui generis. How may this be explained?

How do we receive what are termed "eyewitness reports" from the first century, especially those claimed in gospel writings? What do we make of a personal experience based on an ecstatic vision as described by Paul? As some have portrayed it, revelation is the greatest mystery, although the *fact* of revelation is the greatest certainty; this seems to suggest that ordinary mortals are incapable of fully grasping the processes involved in revelation. Indeed, many of us are hard-pressed to distinguish nonveridical religious experience from a veridical one, especially when there are large numbers of people presumably sharing the same, or a repeated, experience in duration and intensity.

Ultimately, the message from on high rests epistemologically on testimony-giving. Paul had the idea of *ongoing* revelation manifesting itself each time a community of shared faith spoke, i.e., gave testimony of its conviction, inspired by the Holy Spirit. *Anyone* within the community could stand and give witness, and this is what did take place in the first century, from speaking in tongues (languages that were not learned) to ecstatic or frenzied seizures. The picture in *The First Letter of Paul to the Corinthians* 14:26–32 is graphic:

> To sum up, my friends: when you meet for worship, each of you con-
> tributing a hymn, some instruction, a revelation, an ecstatic utterance,
> or its interpretation, see that all of these aim to build up the church.
> If anyone speaks in tongues, only two should speak, or at most three,
> one at a time, and someone must interpret. If there is no interpreter,
> they should keep silent and speak to themselves and to God. . . . If
> someone else present receives a revelation, let the first speaker stop. You
> can all prophesy, one at a time, so that all may receive instruction and
> encouragement.

Testimony-giving under the influence of the Holy Spirit, then, amounted
to truth by *affirmation* and *declaration*. Indeed, church father Bishop Papias
(ca. mid-second century C.E.) preferred oral testimony to the written word:
". . . I did not think that the content of books would profit me as much
as what comes from the living and enduring voice." Accordingly, he collected
sayings and reports from the elderly who might have had contact with
any of the original apostles. These reports were preserved by Papias under
the title *Interpretations of the Sayings of the Lord,* only fragments of
which remain.[6] Out of conviction, one knew that one was speaking or
affirming the truth by announcement: Death had been overcome in the
person of salvation (Yeshua). The *fact* of conviction and a fiery enthusiasm
to ignite others with the flame of that conviction produced truth by
declaration—first oral, then written. In short, this was the process of
conveying the message, as John tells us: "There were many other signs
that Jesus performed in the presence of His disciples, which are not recorded
in this book. Those written here *have* [emphasis added] been recorded
in order that you may believe that Jesus is the Christ, the son of God . . ."
(*The Gospel According to John* 20:30–31).[7]

What Is Not Should Soon Be!

Devotional Literature. Chronicle has, as one of its purposes, the ordering of selected events of the past in a sequential arrangement whether
of topical importance or as pure chronology or precedence. Some view
this as "uncovering the past." Since the human past had ceased to be
of importance, gospel writings were, for the most part, less concerned with
"uncovering the past" than in influencing the present, as may be seen by
an illuminating passage in *The Letter of Paul to the Romans* 15:4–6:

> The scriptures written long ago were all written for our instruction, in
> order that through the encouragment they give us we may maintain our

hope with perseverance. And may the source of all perseverance and all encouragement grant that you may agree with one another after the manner of Christ Jesus, and so with the one mind and one voice you may praise the God and father of our Lord Jesus Christ.

Forcefully, the writer states the purpose of Scripture: It is not to uncover the past as chronological or sequential narrative; rather, it is to offer encouragement in order to stimulate hope, the mainstay of conviction. That some have transposed gospel writings into historiographic summaries is a fact, but that transposition is not based on a purpose discernible within gospel writings themselves. For instance, the many "Lives of Jesus"—as a genre of purported biography—all rest on some imaginative impressions of gospel writings, despite the overt questioning of them as historiography.

In a well-written work entitled *The Prophet from Nazareth,* author Morton Scott Enslin asserted that it is not possible to write a "life of Jesus" because "It has been said and rightly: 'We do not have enough material to write a respectable obituary notice.' " Despite this citation plus the author's own addenda, that gospel writings are dominated by theological and not historical considerations, and that we have no sources upon which to draw, he nevertheless proceeds to reconstruct a life. His justification is that a reconstruction is warranted because critical scholarship does not demand the conclusion that one cannot know *anything* about Jesus (see note 1).

There is no doubt that Enslin has taken as given the affirmations by gospel writings concerning the historicity of a Jesus. He also believes that the gospel portraits are paintings by artisans and artists that permit us to "see the man himself" despite the later composite touches and accretions that were attached thereto. As he puts it: "There is such a thing as the immortality of influence."[8] In contrast, earlier critical writers such as F. C. Baur presented gospel writings as tendentious or partisan literature, and even claimed that Paul's Letters, believed to have been composed far earlier than the gospel writings, were second-century pseudographs. Similarly, the famous David Friedrich Strauss saw only a *suggestion* of history in gospel writings and Bruno Bauer saw none at all. Nevertheless, as Enslin confesses, there is a tendency to rely on the skeleton of gospel "facts" while diverging from the interpretations of them.

It is believed to be far more justifiable to view gospel writings as devotional literature exposing a worshipful attitude, a collection of declarations of personal conviction. As architects and pyramid builders are able to construct monuments and shrines of stone and marble, and as painters do so with dyes and pigments, there are those who are talented in constructing an edifice of verbal materials for the purpose of expressing normative aspirations and inducing reverence toward their pious expression. Pure and simple, gospel writings present themselves as poetic and hopeful summaries of theology and liturgy concerned with a devotional process of conveying the message.

Multiple Traditions. Church fathers tell of the existence of numerous gospels and collected oral traditions. There are gospels of Peter and Thomas, first gospel of James, Ebionite gospel, Nazarene gospel, Hebrew gospel, and Egyptian gospel. Each such gospel presents a complex of what was believed by the particular community in a given locale, the line between dream, wish, and reality being indistinct and blurred. As indicated previously, such traditions were guided not so much by fact as by objective; their vision constructed the past and their objective was to forge a teaching instrument to instruct others in truth, conceived as allegiance to a cause and belief system. A good example of a teaching instrument is *The Gospel* (or *Evangel*) *According to John.* (In a telling comment, Justin Martyr [ca. 150 C.E.] would have preferred the designation "memorabilia of the apostles" to the "Evangel According to. . . .") As is well-known, this very late composition differs considerably in style and content from the three earlier synoptic Gospels of Mark, Matthew, and Luke, so labeled because of their common perspective. *The Gospel According to John* may be seen as a textbook on allegory, mystical allusion, and theosophy; with much theologizing, it is an attempt to unite heaven and earth within one body.

Why was there a multiplicity of gospels in the first place? Traditions, around which communities gathered, were ranked in esteem. Those presumed to be closest to the Master himself in time and place were accorded more singular honor than those more distant from him, hence the preference of some, such as Papias and Ignatius, for the earlier oral tradition over the later written word. Then, too, there were traditions that were preferred in terms of style: the expansive over the simple, the extravagant over the frugal, the wonderful and marvel-centered over the straightforward and humble. These were reflective of differences within recollected claims: from "he was an inspirational teacher" to "he was the anointed one and promised deliverer." In short, there was no *fixed* body of gospel teaching in the first and second centuries. For instance, Papias, a key to primitive Christianity in the post-apostolic age, wrote: "So Matthew copied the Sayings [of Jesus] in the Aramaic language and everyone translated them as well as he could."[9] Each community of believers came to regard itself as a co-equal witness in bearing testimony to a truth believed to be timeless and enduring. Much excavation would be needed to uncover what later mound lay on top of earlier strata, how simple occurrence became prophecy through transpositions of time: a common characteristic of memory, as it ranges over the events of a lifetime. As Mircea Eliade reminds us, collective memory is ahistorical; it annuls history and transforms events.[10]

As a result of the multiplicity of traditions, there came the need to bring together an authoritative version of collected traditions to which the faithful could subscribe, a canon or official document, setting forth self-definition. This became known as Scripture and was the authentic account and description of what was to become common doctrine. Obviously, a centralizing tendency with a political form had come into being to integrate the multiple communities into a unit professing a commonly held conviction. Henceforth, the existence of multiple gospels was not to be considered evidence of conflicting testimony but rather as proof of the diffusion of testimony in a variety of *forms,* perhaps in much the same way that multiple languages offer testimony for the diffusion of common thought and common knowledge. By the third century C.E., twenty-seven written documents came to be regarded as authentic Scripture.

It is somewhat difficult for us in the twentieth century to appreciate the significance of a *book* in the two centuries before the common era. If one wanted to speak authoritatively, one *had* to have a book. This seal of approval went back at least half a millennium if not more. In the seventh precentury, it was the discovery of a scroll of writing that told King Josiah (Yeho-shi-yahu, "Yahu Saves") that the written word is truth (2 Chronicles 34:14). In the interpretation of the prophetess Ḥuldah, who was consulted by the king (2 Kings 22:8–20), the scroll contained revealed wisdom from on high and could brook no disagreement. In the two centuries before the common era, "hidden books" were composed under pseudonyms and assigned to authorship by famous personages (pseudepigrapha), e.g., the Book of Enoch and the Testaments of the Twelve Patriarchs. Not only did the assigned authorship increase credibility and authenticity, it also was in the accepted tradition of a respected king of Judah, as indicated in 2 Chronicles 34:14: ". . . the priest Ḥilkiah discovered the Scroll of the Law of YHVH given by Moses," that hitherto "lost works" could be rediscovered. It was within this matrix of tradition that New Testament writings were born. If there is a book, it *has* to be true, since it was revealed by God to man.[11] When Muhammed referred to "People of the Book," he was indicating that the people possessed divine warrant or revealed truth; what was written was dictated by God. In consequence, *he* became inspired to record visions and messages dictated by the archangel. The writings or book became certification of an epiphany such as Paul is said to have experienced. When epiphanies through the written word began to proliferate, distinctions had to be made between the canonical and noncanonical, authorized versions and nonauthorized ones. For Jews, *all* of the intertestamental literature, excluding

Daniel, became apocryphal (truly hidden), while for the later church, many of the works produced between the two testaments became canonical. The intertestamental literature may, in fact, be regarded as pre-Christian or pro-Christian sources.

"Let the Scriptures Be Fulfilled." Inquiry or investigation in the twentieth century involves the verification or the refutation of hypotheses that purport to test some theory; the verdict can go in either direction. One cannot speak this way in referring to a theory of knowing in the first century. For the judgments of objectivity and truth were then being erected by a brotherhood upon a basic premise that was not subject to doubt at all: the Redeemer rose from death. With that conviction as a postulate, there was no question remotely possible that a life had not been lived. Yet, what was believed to be external substantiation was required—external, that is, to individual affirmation, the "I believe" of the adherent. The solid testimony of an inspired source was needed. That source was obviously the writings already in existence of earlier prophets and the songs of praise known as the psalms, contained in the Greek translation of the Bible called the Septuagint, an Alexandrian product of the mid-third century B.C.E. This document was read less as the national history of Israel and more as a book of evidence concerning salvation (*yeshua*) as residing in a person. It was interpreted as oracle and prediction of an event that was to usher in the redemption of all humanity; its individual verses were thoroughly and exhaustively combed in the effort to discover and secure elements of substantiation. Under what may be characterized as a coherence theory of truth, diffuse elements in the form of what were held to be predictions or, at least, future-oriented declarations, were assembled and connected by the theme of redemption, which was taken as a given.

Thus, in the detailed scrutiny of these existing sources and their interpretation as demonstrable justifications, the certifying sources themselves were labeled the "Old" Testament or Covenant, the clear implication being that a new covenant could be expected. The old covenant or testament was but a prologomenon to a new announcement; i.e., the certifying source itself was read and comprehended as pure prediction, to be superseded by a new edition, containing the actual fulfillment. This new edition, *because* it demonstrated the authenticity and veracity of the old, was thereby more important and more authoritative as Scripture. As stated in *The Second Letter of Paul to the Corinthians* (5:17): "So if anyone is in Christ there is a new creation, everything old has passed away, see everything has become new." "Let the Scriptures Be Fulfilled" was, then, a remarkable exclamatory formula: it combined a mode of investigation together with the findings thereof. The fulfillment was the new Scripture!

Applications of the Formula

Extravagant Praise. Extravagance was very common in oral tradition, and the role of exaggeration or hyperbole and redundance were seen as natural. In Hebrew liturgy we read an extract of a prayer for rain:

> Though our mouths were filled with song as the sea [with water] and our tongues with melody as the roaring waves, our lips full of praise as the expanse of the heavens, and though our eyes were to shine as the sun or moon . . . we would still be unable to offer thanks to you, our God, to bless your name for "one thousandth of the countless millions of favors" which you have conferred on us. (Talmud Berakhoth 59b)

In a land subject to periodic drought and extreme dependence on lifegiving rain, each raindrop can be seen as a distinct favor, hence, "countless millions of favors" begins to make sense beyond simple overstatement.

What may be regarded as redundance today was fairly common in first and second-century Judaean thought and expression. To magnify God meant to use multiple adjectives in the hopes that *one* might be applicable. Since God was a unique Being, human expression inevitably fell short in glorifying and proclaiming the fullness of his spirit, so one had to repeat oneself variously. Consequently, the longer the list of adjectives, the more praiseworthy. In the Hebrew doxology known as the Kaddish, this becomes evident: "Blessed, praised, glorified and exalted, extolled, honored and adored and lauded be the name of the Holy One, blessed is He, though He is beyond all blessings and hymns, praises and adorations that are ever uttered in the world. . . ."

Now, if this style of expression is taken as description of an *event* or occurrence, such as contained in gospel testimonies, one can begin to see how hyperbole and redundance become meritorious: the longer the list of adjectives or the more magnificent and marvelous the descriptions, the greater and more *valid* is the testimony that is being offered. The testimonials that we hear at formal gatherings such as the introductions of a famous speaker or the honoring of a recipient of an award or the eulogies expressed at funerals are somewhat similar. The longer the list of attainments and words of praise employed to describe the individual, the greater the honor that accrues, and the *stronger the testimony* being offered.

The Encomium. There was a style of biographical writing in the first centuries of the common era known as encomiastic, or fullsome praise only.

According to Aristotle, it was the duty of the encomiast to omit the negative in his characterization or description of an individual (*Rhetoric* I.ix.33). As already suggested, we immediately recognize the encomiast or eulogist at work at a testimonial dinner or in introducing the recipient of an honorary academic degree.

An example of the ecomiastic style has been associated with the third-century C.E. writer Philostratus, who was commissioned by the wife of a Roman emperor to record the life of Apollonius of Tyana, a first-century holy man. Philostratus's hagiographic treatment of this celebrated figure—a blend of fact and fancy—elevated Apollonius into a formidable adversary to the historical claims of a nascent Christianity. If one reads Philostratus's account of the trial of Apollonius before the Emperor Domitian (81–96 C.E.), one sees an inordinate love of rhetoric. A lengthy, sparkling speech is made by Apollonius, not so much to substantiate his defense or to refute a charge as to demonstrate the skill of the writer, Philostratus, who composed the speech. Credibility becomes strained in the face of an almost theatrical atmosphere of pure invention or blending of objective fact with subjective fancy. And yet, it may be that the period (and place) was given to the dramatization of the ordinary, with biography conceived as hagiology. An author remarks: "In a sense, the lives of Moses or Apollonius or Pythagoras or Jesus were written as handbooks of moral perfection."[12] It may, however, be countered that the authors *themselves* (Philo of Alexandria or Philostratus) were not considered holy instruments inspired by revelation.

Reconstructions. This writing mode ranged all the way from the free invention of encomium to the blurring of chronologic distinctions. The differentiative lines between the temporal concepts of *then* and *now* were often treated as purely artificial constructions that could be contracted or dispensed with at will; indeed, in casual conversation, one may speak of then and now as if they are identical. The spatial concepts of *here* and *there,* too, were often collapsed as identical, or simply viewed as obstacles that interfere with pure *knowing,* i.e, conviction of the truth (regarding redemption). Differentiations, so important to scientific understanding, were seen as less than helpful or as hindrances. Thus, it was not uncommon for events to become telescoped, particularly when collective memory operated. A happening of an earlier century or in a different place could easily be transported across the fiction of chronologic differentiation to explain the present, or a current occurrence could be sent back "in time" retrojectively to become a prediction. The annulment of time distinctions, or its fixing, occurs in the process of thought known as hypostatization.

Chapter 13 of *The Gospel According to Mark* contains material illustrative of the transporting of events from one time "zone" to another, the telescoping of *then* and *now,* from *there* to *here.* In verse 4, the disciples ask: "What will be the sign that all these things are about to be fulfilled?" Jesus replies: "These are the first birth-pangs of the new age" (v. 8), and a significant parenthetical expression follows: "Be on your guard; I have forewarned you of it all." This admonition occurs four times within the thirty-seven verses of chapter 13 (vv. 5, 19, 23, 33) wherein is contained a lengthy peroration on the end of an age.

In verse 14, one finds a curious reference: "But when you see 'the abomination of desolation' usurping a place which is not his . . . then those who are in Judaea must take to the hills." This enigmatic statement can be traced back to Daniel 11:31, which is a reference to the Seleuc[k]id ruler Antiochus IV in 175 B.C.E. When the king established altars to Zeus within Judaea, Maccabean guerrillas were "taking to the hills." Daniel 11:31 reads: "Soldiers in his command will desecrate the sanctuary and citadel; they will abolish the regular offering and will set up the abominable thing that causes desolation." Then, in Daniel 12:11, the text reads: "From the time when the regular offering is abolished and the 'abomination of desolation' is set up, one thousand, two hundred and ninety days will elapse."

The curious reference in Daniel to the "abominable thing of desolation" has to do with the blasphemous act of King Antiochus IV, later to be repeated by the Roman Emperor Caligula (37–41 C.E.), who wanted to have *his* statue erected in the Temple at Jerusalem. In *The Second Letter of Paul to the Thessalonians* 2:4, there is reference to "the final rebellion against God: "He is the adversary who raises himself up against every so-called god or object of worship and even enthrones himself in God's temple, claiming to be God." This may be pointed at Caligula's bold move to have his statue worshipped, and Daniel 11:36 avers that "The King will do as he pleases; he will exalt and magnify himself above every god and against the God of gods he will utter monstrous blasphemies."

Since Daniel was written in the second century B.C.E., it seems that the incident relating to the acts of Antiochus IV (175 B.C.E.) is fresh in the mind of the writer, although the same book refers back to events occurring in the late sixth century B.C.E., e.g., Belshazzar's banquet. What seems apparent in all of the above is that transpositions, retrojections, and projections were part of what was considered natural writing style, and thus to be imitated. It does not then appear as surprising to find the phrase "the abomination of desolation" being lifted right out of one work and stitched into that of another (Mark 13:14 and Matthew 24:15–16) with a new ascription of utterance.

Thus, part of the reconstructive or elaborative process with textual material involved the splicing together of various scriptural verses to form a composite idea. Thematic material such as "the end of days," "salvation," and individual survival beyond the grave lent themselves readily to the search for appropriate supports. In fact, such splicings of scriptural verses became the basis of hortatory teaching as well as liturgical invocations and hymnody.

Gap-Filling. A feature of the reconstruction of material was the practice of interpolation or gap-filling, i.e., clarifications and explications introduced into a narrative. This involved much creative insight and the ingenuity of elaboration on associated ideas; similarities sometimes become identities. There was an interplay between oral traditions and their interpretation in order to make the scriptures more complete, the reality being that the words of God endure forever. As the formula in the New Testament puts it: "All this happened in order to fulfill what the Lord declared through the prophet" (Matthew 1:22). What follows is a detailing of two exemplars, one in the Old Testament and the other in gospel narratives. We begin with two versions of the reign of King Manasseh of Judah, one from 2 Kings and the other from 2 Chronicles.[13] (Textual differences are italicized.)

2 KINGS 21	2 CHRONICLES 33
v. 1: Manasseh was twelve years old when he began to reign and he reigned fifty and five years in Jerusalem *and his mother's name was Ḥeftzi-bah.*	v. 1. Manasseh was twelve years old when he began to reign and he reigned fifty and five years in Jerusalem.
v. 6: And he made his son to pass through the fire and practiced soothsaying and used enchantments . . . he wrought such provocative evil in YHVH's eyes.	v. 6: And he also made his *children* to pass through the fire *in the valley of the son of Hinnom* and he practiced soothsaying and used enchantments . . . he wrought much evil in the sight of YHVH to provoke *Him.*
v. 7: And he set the image of the Asherah that he had made, in the House of which YHVH said to David* and to Solomon his son. . . . I will put My name forever. *David is spelled here Dvd.	v. 7: And he set the *graven* image of the idol which he made in the *house of God* of which Elohim [God] said to David* and to Solomon his son . . . I will put my name forever. *David is spelled here Dvyd.

v. 8: And I will no longer cause the foot of Israel to wander out of the land which I gave to their fathers, if only they will observe to do according to all that I have commanded them and according to all the Law that my servant Moses commanded them.

v. 8: And I will no longer *remove* the foot of Israel from *off the land* which I appointed to *your* fathers, if only they will observe to do all that I have commanded them, *all the laws and statutes and ordinances by the hand of Moses.*

v. 9: But they did not listen and Manasseh seduced them to do evil . . .

v. 9: *And Manasseh seduced Judah and the inhabitants of Jerusalem* to do evil . . .

It may be noted that the differences or changes in the text of Chronicles are more or less minor, although not entirely insignificant, and they reveal the process of textual explication. In the verses which now follow may be seen a major amplification and interpolation:

2 KINGS 21

2 CHRONICLES 33

v. 16: And also, Manasseh shed much innocent blood till he had filled Jerusalem from one end to another, apart from his sin wherewith he made Judah to sin in the sight of YHVH.

v. 12: And when he was in distress he sought out YHVH his God and humbled himself greatly before the God of his fathers. And he prayed to him and was entreated of him and he heard his supplication and brought him back to Jerusalem to his kingdom. Then Manasseh knew that YHVH was God. [Verses 15–17 describe the penitential acts of King Manasseh.]

v. 17: And the rest of the doings of Manasseh and all that he did and his sin, are they not written in the book of the Chronicles of the kings of Judah?

v. 18: And the rest of the days of Manasseh *and his prayer unto God and the words of the seers who spoke to him in the name of YHVH, the God of Israel,* behold they are among the acts of the Kings of *Israel.*

It will be observed that verse 12 in 2 Chronicles has no counterpart in 2 Kings. It is something entirely new. Second Chronicles 33:18 then refers back to what is related in verse 12. Here we see how a later pious receiver of a tradition could not permit the sin of the king of Judah to persist without expiation. So the writer of the Chronicles tells of a repentant Manasseh who confesses his sins and makes atonement for them, thereby receiving pardon and restoration. Pious imagination adds new features to make the story more complete: "what might have been" guides the narrative of the writers of the Chronicles; i.e., repentance can be made even for grievous sins. However, one does not know whether the story actually happened as described.

We turn now to view the gap-filling process in a selection from the New Testament. In *The Gospel According to Matthew* 26: 36–44 we read:

> Jesus then came with his disciples to a place called Gethsemane, and he said to them, "Sit here while I go over there to pray." He took with him Peter and the two sons of Zebedee. Distress and anguish overwhelmed him and he said to them, "My heart is ready to break with grief. Stop here and stay awake with me." Then he went on a little farther, threw himself down, and prayed, "My Father, if it is possible, let this cup pass me by. Yet not my will but yours."
>
> He came back to the disciples and found them asleep; and he said to Peter, "What! Could none of you stay awake with me for one hour? Stay awake and pray that you may be spared the test. The spirit is willing but the flesh is weak."
>
> He went away a second time and prayed: "My Father, if it is not possible for this cup to pass me by without my drinking it, your will be done." He came again and found them asleep, for their eyes were heavy. So he left them and went away again and prayed a third time, using the same words as before.

From this account, it is obvious that Jesus prayed in solitude while his disciples slept. How does it happen that the substance and style of the prayer are known to us? For a response, we have to turn to *The Gospel According to Luke,* 22:39–46:

> Then he went out and made his way as usual to the mount of Olives, accompanied by the disciples. When he reached the place he said to them, "Pray that you may be spared the test." He himself withdrew from them about a stone's throw, knelt down, and began to pray: "Father, if it be your will, take this cup from me. Yet not my will but yours be done."
>
> *And now there appeared to him an angel from heaven bringing him strength, and in anguish of spirit he prayed the more urgently; and his sweat was like drops of blood falling to the ground* [emphasis added].
>
> When he rose from prayer and came to the disciples he found them

asleep, *worn out by grief.* "Why are you sleeping?" he said. "Rise and pray that you may be spared the test."

We can note the gap-filling by the author of Luke. With the disciples asleep, the prayer of Jesus as well as his anguish and physical condition require some explanation. So, an angel notes his physical condition and records the words of prayer; an explanation is also offered for the slumber of the disciples.

It was incomprehensible that such an important event should go undetailed, let alone unreported. To sketch in details under holy inspiration is merely to complete what was skeletal. Energized by grace and heavenly blessings, the scriptural writers were under God's dictation; their scribal efforts were not their own.

Sometimes the attempt at gap-filling raises other questions, but here there is only concern with the *process* of creative amplification as clarification. One further brief illustration will suffice.

The above story continues with the arrest of Jesus who is interrogated at a hearing in the house of the high priest. At this turn of events, *The Gospels According to Mark and Matthew* tell us that "the disciples all deserted him and ran away" (Mark 14:50 and Matthew 26:56). Again, an obvious question can be raised: How is it that we know the nature of the questions asked (and the answers thereunto) at the hearing held in the house of the high priest? *The Gospel According to Matthew* 26:59 tells us that: "The chief priests and the whole Council tried to find some allegation against Jesus that would warrant a death sentence; but they failed to find one, though many came forward with false evidence." (See also Mark 14:55,56.)

At this point, gap-filling is less elaborate. *The Gospel According to Luke* 22:54–71 relates only that Peter followed at a distance and remained outside in the courtyard. In addition, *The Gospel According to John* 18:15,19 is only mildly suggestive:

> Jesus was followed by Simon Peter and another disciple. This disciple, who was known to the high priest, went with Jesus into the high priest's courtyard, but Peter stayed outside at the door. . . . The high priest questioned Jesus about his disciples and about his teaching.

Presumably, the details of the hearing were recounted by the "disciple who was known to the high priest." In this instance, the gap-filling is not as complete as one might like to have it. "What might have been" became the author.

*　*　*

Typologies. Since the Old Testament was viewed oracularly, that is as an introduction to the New, it was consulted for typological components. Premonitions, foreshadowings, prefigurings, and preliminary sketches constitute such components.[14] To first- and second-century thought, not only was there nothing unusual in this procedure, it was typical. Complete revelations were given only to the chosen few, e.g., the selection of Paul as an apostle. More common were partial epiphanies, the seeing of *an* aspect of the whole, the finished construction remaining for others to complete. Thus, the Old Testament was only an introductory revelation, anticipating and awaiting the post-Sinaitic, newer edition for comprehensibility and completion. Scenes within the Old Testament could be seen as raw material calling for explication and embellished narrative. Presented here are two likely episodes, incidents from the eleventh to tenth century B.C.E. and the seventh century B.C.E., as exemplars of typological material.

The first episode, revealing the framework for narrative expansion, is found in the life of David, king of Israel. One could read the Book of 2 Samuel 15:1–19:24, relating an account of the rebellion of David's son, Absalom (Avshalom), purely as literal narrative, occurring only once. It is here suggested, however, that the narrative contains typological material, permitting reproduction within another structure. The context of the four chapters is the rebellion of a son (the prince) against his father (the king). This particular king (David), a Meshiaḥ, is the typology of an anointed one to come—in Greek translation, Christos. Ultimately the rebellion is crushed, but for the moment the king is driven from his throne by the proclamation of his son that he (Absalom/Avshalom) is king (2 Samuel 15:10).

David prepares to abandon the city of Jerusalem, for he fears an attack from the south, the operational base seized by his son, the former capital at Hebron (Ḥevron). Second Samuel 15:30 records David retiring from the city: he went by way of the Mount of Olives, weeping and with covered head, and the people with him wept, too, as they crossed over the Kidron Brook. In David's camp, there was a traitor by the name of Aḥitophel, who later hangs himself (2 Samuel 17:23). As David continues on his retreat from the city, a descendant of the House of Saul—Shimi ben Gera—curses him and throws stones at him (2 Samuel 16:5–7). David's army commander, Abishai (Avishai), wants to kill Shimi for daring to revile and curse God's anointed. Indeed, Shimi taunts and derides the fleeing David; in his hour of humiliation, with his own son trying to wrest the kingdom from him, he is subjected to contempt and scorn.

Here is a framework for script revision of principal characters. The locale is at the Mount of Olives in the foregoing narrative; the Passion narrative of Mark 14:26 begins with a crossover to the Mount of Olives. David represents Jesus, and Ahitophel, the conspirator, becomes Judas, the traitor who, like Ahitophel, hangs himself for his betrayal (Matthew 27:3–5). Shimi, the reviler, represents some of the rabble who abuse Jesus (Matthew 26:67). Abishai (Avishai), man of the sword, is the model for the character in *The Gospel According to Matthew* 26:51, who cuts off the ear of the servant of the high priest. Jesus restrains him: "Put up your sword. All who take the sword die by the sword." The scene seems to reconstruct 2 Samuel 16:9–10, where the intemperate man of the sword, Abishai (Avishai), declares: "Why let this dead dog curse my lord, the king? Let me go over and take off his head." To which David replies:

> What has this to do with us, you sons of Zeruiah? [Abishai and his brother Joab, known for their violent tempers.] . . . If my very own son is out to kill me, who can wonder at this Benjaminite. Let him be, let him curse, for YHVH has told him to. Perhaps YHVH will mark my suffering and bestow a blessing upon me in place of the curse laid on me this day. (2 Samuel 16:11–12)

David, whose hands were bloody from war, here repudiates violence. Jesus, of course, is presented as pacific to begin with, but he declares: "Do you suppose that I cannot appeal for help to my Father, and at once be sent more than twelve legions of angels? But how then would the scriptures be fulfilled which say that this must happen?" (Matthew 26:53–54).

The reply seems a variation of "let him curse, for YHVH has told him to"; indeed, the outlines of the story of one thousand years earlier is discernible. Tradition does not alter in content, only in form. The old tale is reinterpreted and reapplied, with the core preserved, i.e., the theme of divine governance and recompense. In the preservation and recasting of fragments of incidents we can see that ". . . this has all happened to fulfill what the prophets wrote" (Matthew 26:56).

The second episode, from the seventh century B.C.E., appears in Jeremiah (Yirmi-yahu) 26:9, where the prophet is threatened with death for delivering a message of doom about the destruction of the "house" [Temple] and the city [Jerusalem]: "This house shall be like Shiloh, and this city shall be desolate, without an inhabitant." In *The Gospel According to Mark* 13:2, a similar message is set forth with regard to the Second Temple: "Not one stone will be left upon another; they will all be thrown down." This is repeated by Luke 19:41: "When he came in sight of the city, he wept over it . . . your enemies . . . will not leave you one stone standing on another. . . ."

Jeremiah (Yirmi-yahu) 26:15 continues: ". . . if you put me to death, you and this city will be guilty of murdering an innocent man; for truly it was YHVH who sent me to say all this to you." Somehow, this seemed to have a restraining effect and the threat to his life abated. However, at the same time there was another who also spoke in the name of God, Uriah, son of Shema-yahu: "He prophesied against this city and this land, just as Jeremiah had done. King Yeho-yakim . . . sought to put him to death. On hearing of this, Uriah fled in fear to Egypt. King Yeho-yakim dispatched men to fetch Uriah from Egypt. When they brought him to the king, he had him put to the sword . . ." (Jeremiah 26:20–23).

It may be noted that the fragment of a flight to Egypt reappears in *The Gospel According to Matthew* 2:13: ". . . an angel of the Lord appeared to Joseph in a dream and said, 'Get up, take the child and his mother and escape with them to Egypt . . . for [King] Herod is going to search for the child to kill him.' "

The elements of the trial of Jeremiah (Yirmi-yahu) and the execution of Uriah, fetched from Egypt at royal command, remained deep within the cultural memory to form the free-floating material from which a later narrative could be constructed.

Pseudonymity. An extension of the reconstructive and typological applications of "Let the Scriptures Be Fulfilled" may be seen in the use of pseudonyms and pseudepigraphy. Whole books were authored by what is referred to in the twentieth century as a ghost writer, and then retrojected across a time "zone." For instance, in the work known as Ecclesiasticus, a second-century B.C.E. writer claimed kinship with the tenth century B.C.E. as son of King Solomon. Other works, written in the period between 200 B.C.E. and 200 C.E. (e.g., 1 and 2 Esdras), consisting of poetry, proverbs, sayings, and stories, were attached to honored names from the past; this added the weight of their prestige to the new creation that was usually an expansion on, or elaboration of, an oft-repeated theme. It was within this matrix of tradition, referred to as Intertestamental Literature, that New Testament writings were developed.

Summary: Conveying the Message

It may be seen that the entire process of *conveying the message* was conceptualized as fulfillment of the Divine Will. In the words of the Hebrew doxology (see note 1), ". . . in the world which he created according to his will 'Let his kingdom Come.' " Thus, the Scriptures were theography; profound and pregnant with meaning, they molded the significance of all human events. In very early periods of human development, sympathetic magical acts were performed in the primitive supposition that events on earth could influence or, at least, imitate happenings in the cosmos. Seemingly, control over one's thoughts permitted a corresponding control over things; as Sir James Frazer put it, the *order* of ideas was mistaken for the order of nature.[15] The obverse is that events in heaven could influence those on earth—by fiat or declaration. Hence, messages for *now* were sought in earlier events, *as if* known heretofore by an Adam or Enoch. Similarly, inferences were made from *here* to *there* by juxtaposition, fluid association, and connection. Very often, *what might have been* became the author since one was simply engaged in helping to fulfill the Divine Will. It is then understandable why it was the vogue to ascribe later writings (200 B.C.E. to 200 C.E.) on *origins and ends* to earlier biblical characters. Considered as ongoing revelations, these apocalyptic tales, stories, legends, and traditions were expressions of hope for a new beginning on earth. Thus, the "testimonies" of a new beginning were an ongoing folk composition, or an epic-type synthesis of ideas, methodology, and hermeneutics.[16] They reveal the artistic endeavor of gap-filling, typological reconstruction, and continual amplification and elaboration to make the event or the saying(s) about an earthly kingdom more and more complete.

It was also the vogue for a student or disciple to bear testimony to his teacher in a stylistic formula to insure authenticity, and to reassure that what was being transmitted was, indeed, "received from the Teacher himself." In this regard, the expression of bishop Papias (ca. 120 C.E.) may be noted:

> When Mark became Peter's interpreter, he wrote down, though by no means verbatim, as much as he accurately remembered of the words and works of the Lord; for he had neither heard the Lord nor been in his company; but he subsequently joined Peter, as I said. Now, Peter did not intend to give a complete exposition of the Lord's ministry, but delivered his instructions to meet the needs of the moment. It follows, then, that Mark was guilty of no blunder if he wrote, simply to the best of his recollections, an incomplete account.[17]

It is to be remembered that Mark is the earliest of the synoptic Gospels and that Matthew and Luke were attempts to make Mark "more complete." In this general fashion, the collective testimonies *became gospels* to reveal a blending of and connection to the world above and the world below: "Thy will be done on earth as it is in heaven." *This* was the image that determined the content of the testimonies themselves, ultimately to be compressed within such popular creedal affirmations as the Lord's Prayer.

Perhaps the best vessel and medium for containing and conveying the message of "Thy Will Be Done on Earth," was the Passion story itself. Without *that* narrative there is no faith community, for its historicity is dependent upon its being reexperienced. If viewed as a pedagogic instrument representing a recapitulation of all the elements of that brilliant formula of "Let the Scriptures Be Fulfilled," one can come to appreciate the power and influence of gospel writings.

In an age before cinema, radio, and television, the stage was a prime medium for transmission of ideas and explanation of what was deemed to be reality itself. Thus, one can see in the Passion story a successor to the great mystery plays, which served as magical art from time immemorial throughout the Near East. When viewed as drama, the gospel treatment of the Passion becomes more translucent than if read purely as historiographic narrative.

The action-packed story takes place within a single twenty-four-hour time span, beginning with a farewell supper at evening and ending with a cultic human sacrifice in the shape of a capital execution fifteen hours later. Within this brief compass of time, there are powerful punctuating climaxes, together with characteristically sudden shifts of scene and episodes: a ceremonial supper is followed by solitary prayer and agonizing soliloquy in a garden; then comes a dramatic betrayal and arrest scene, a night-hearing, an early-morning trial at a governor's office; a crowd gathers and shouts—ostensibly in condemnation—"Bar Abbas"[18] (Son of the Father) instead of what it had shouted a day earlier, "Hosanna" (Save Us); then comes a climactic portrayal of a solemn cortege to a place of sacrificial execution; the final scene includes a three-to-six-hour process of painful expiration, followed by entombment and subsequent ascension and apotheosis. Whether intended or not, one sees in the textual presentations the characteristics of drama and its division into acts and scenes. That the presentations subsequently became a "passion play" may be a coincidence, but a highly suggestive one that it was so intended from the outset. The drama is such a success that we believe it is *at least* a historical occurrence, if not a cosmic event or theophany that is taking place in the *here and now*.

Notes

The Kingdom of God

1. The doxology known as the Kaddish expresses fervent hope for the sovereignty of God's kingdom on earth and is set forth in the future tense:

Yitgadal veyitkadash shemey rabba b'olma di v'ra khirutey veyamlikh malkhutey, veytazmaḥ purkaney vikarev meshiḥey, . . . baagala uvizeman kariv. . . .

Let God's great name be hallowed and magnified in the world whose creation he willed. May his kingdom be realized and let his deliverance blossom forth and his anointed one draw near . . . soon in your lifetime. . . .

Although there is no explicit reference here to death, in the Jewish tradition, the doxology is recited by mourners upon bereavement. One can see how this doxology could be transmuted into a Christological interpretation of victory over death by a grammatical turn, the future tense being converted into a past tense: His kingdom *has* come and redemption *has* sprouted forth in the person of his anointed one.

2. F. C. Conybeare (trans.), "The Treatise of Eusebius" in *Philostratus: The Life of Apollonius of Tyana,* vol. 2 (Cambridge: Harvard University Press, 1948), pp. 191, 493.

3. All citations from the Bible, particularly the New Testament writings, are from *The Revised English Bible* (Oxford University Press, Cambridge University Press, 1989).

Divine Knowledge: A Gift Bestowed Upon the Chosen

4. Julian Huxley, *Religion Without Revelation* (New York: New American Library), 1957, p. 86.

5. Rudolf Bultmann, *Jesus Christ and Mythology* (New York: Charles Scribner's Sons, 1958), p. 16.

6. Bishop Papias of Hieropolis in Phrygia was a disciple of St. John the Apostle. Ca. 130–140 C.E., he compiled five books, *Interpretations of Sayings of the Lord,* culled from the oral testimony of the elderly. While the work has largely disappeared and only fragments remain, it was of importance to later Christian writers up to the ninth century. What Papias had to say about the origins of *The Gospels According to Mark and Matthew* was very valuable, and some of the content is recoverable from such writers as St. Jerome (fifth century) and Bishop Photius of Constantinople in the ninth century. See Edgar J. Goodspeed, *The Apostolic Fathers* (New York: Harper and Brothers, 1950), Fragment 2, #4, p. 265. Translation based on the Funk-Bihlmeyer edition, vol. 1, published at Tübingen, 1924.

Ignatius, second bishop of Antioch after St. Peter, expressed something similar to Papias. Apostolic doctrine was all-important to him, but it was of little consequence whether it was written or oral. See Robert M. Grant, *The Apostolic Fathers,* vol. 1 (New York: Thomas Nelson and Sons, 1964, p. 62.

7. It is clear from this statement by John that gospel writings were guided as much by purpose as by oral testimony. The writings reflected the declarations

and affirmations of the compilers themselves *about themselves* to serve as models for the "right belief" of others.

What Is Not Should Soon Be!

8. "It is indeed impossible to reconstruct a life or biography of Jesus of Nazareth; . . . it is entirely possible to gain a very clear picture of the sort of man he was. . . . Not only is it possible; it is well worth the doing. The critics have not taken away the actual Jesus of history. What they have done is to show the unreality of the Jesus who has been superficially read out of the Gospels, transformed into the glorified image and likeness of each generation which has attempted so to do, and then read back again into the Gospel pages. That Jesus has vanished. The critics have not destroyed him. They have simply shown that he never existed" (Morton S. Enslin, *The Prophet From Nazareth* [New York: McGraw-Hill Book Company, 1961], pp. 4, 6, 9).

9. Edgar J. Goodspeed, *The Apostolic Fathers* (New York: Harper and Brothers, 1950), p. 265.

10. Mircea Eliade, *Cosmos and History* (New York: Harper and Row, Torchbook Edition, 1959), p. 46.

11. In an examination of the earliest Christian books (before 400 C.E.), the author is concerned with the materials of reproducing the writings. He concludes that, for the most part, they were simple and practical, in some cases, written on "discarded scratch paper." ". . . [t]he form in which they [the writings] appeared was a product of the vital moral and religious spirit which in some two centuries conquered the Roman Empire" (C. C. McCown, "The Earliest Christian Books," in *The Biblical Archaeologist Reader,* ed. D. N. Freedman and G. E. Wright [Garden City, N.Y.: Doubleday, Anchor Books, 1961], p. 261).

Applications of the Formula

12. David R. Cartlidge and David L. Dungan, *Documents for the Study of the Gospels* (Cleveland: William Collins Publishers, 1989), p. 273.

13. *The Holy Scriptures According to the Masoretic Text* (Philadelphia: Jewish Publication Society, 1964).

14. The man of God's announcement to the mother of Samson, the Nazirite, "You shall conceive and bear a son . . . and he shall begin to save Israel . . ." (Judges 13:3,7), is an example of a preliminary sketch. The Annunciation scene by the angel Gabriel to Mary, ". . . you will conceive and give birth to a son, and you are to give him the name Jesus [Savior]" (Luke 1:31), seems to echo the sketch of Judges 13.

Summary: Conveying the Message

15. James G. Frazer, *The Golden Bough,* abr. ed. (New York: Macmillan Company, 1951), p. 121.

16. The fairly late *Testimony Book* of St. Epiphanius (315–403 C.E.) is revealing. From the following excerpt, one comes to understand the concept of "testimony" that was operative in the fourth century C.E.:

> By the holy and blessed EPIPHANIUS Archbishop of Constantia in Cyprus TESTIMONIES of the divinely inspired and holy scriptures concerning the coming from heaven to earth—of the only Word of God and the miracles wrought through him and his passion and resurrection and his second and future appearing.
> 1 That before the ages the Son was begotten
> 2 That he was with the Father—
> 3 That he was the joint creator—
> 4 That he was sent out—
> 5 That he would come—. . . . (*A Pseudo-Epiphanius Testimony Book* [The Society of Biblical Literature, University of Montana, Scholars Press, 1974], p. 9).

17. "The Fragments of Papias," in *The Didache or the Teaching of the Twelve Apostles,* trans. James A. Kleist (Westminster, Md.: Newman Press, 1948), p. 118; Fragment 2, #15 of "Interpretations of Sayings of the Lord."

Eusebius's statement concerning the writings of Mark is worthy of note:

> In this way the tidings of God came to dwell among the Romans . . .
> The light of faith grew so radiant in the hearts of those who listened to Peter that it was not enough for them to have heard him only once. They were not satisfied to receive the doctrine of the divine Revelation from unwritten testimony alone. With numerous entreaties they begged Mark, whose Gospel is extant [Eusebius lived 264–340 C.E.] and who was a companion of Peter, to leave a written memoir of the doctrine which had been preached to them; nor did they cease until they had persuaded him. Thus they were responsible for the writing of what is known as the Gospel according to Mark. (*The Ecclesiastical History, H.E.* II, 15:1–2 in Colm Luibhéid, *The Essential Eusebius* [New York: The New American Library, 1966], p. 80).

In *H.E.* III.39, Eusebius reproduces some of the materials of Papias of Heirapolis (ca. 130 C.E.) and adds some comments of his own:

> And the same writer [Papias] has quoted other things also, as coming to him from unwritten tradition; for instance, certain strange parables of the Saviour and teachings of His, and some other things of a rather mythical character. . . .
> For he [Papias] evidently was a man of exceedingly small

intelligence, as one might say judging from his discourses; nevertheless it was owing to him that so very many churchmen after him adopted a like opinion, taking their stand on the fact that he was a man of primitive times . . ." (Cited from *A New Eusebius,* ed. J. Stevenson [London: Holy Trinity Church, 1957], p. 51).

It appears that Papias is a very important source to Eusebius and, indeed, to the early Church, but Fragment 2, #15, concerning the quality of Mark's recollections which make up *The Gospel According to Mark,* seems to be something of an embarrassment to the learned Bishop of Caesarea.

18. Philo of Alexandria wrote ca. 40 C.E. about King Agrippa II, the last nominal ruler of Judea and personal friend of Emperor Claudius. He relates how Agrippa was insulted at Alexandria by a crowd that received the encouragement of the Prefect of Alexandria and Egypt, Flaccus. Circa 37 C.E., a lunatic was dressed as a mock king and made sport of, while the mockery was aimed at Agrippa. The name of the mock king was *Carabas.*

The relevance of this incident is the date 37 C.E., the mock king who was called "Lord," and the name *Carabas.* (See Matthew 27:28,29.) The similarity to the details of the Passion Story (Barabas) suggest a common source:

"There was a certain lunatic named Carabas. . . . The rioters drove the poor fellow into the gymnasium and set him up on high to be seen of all and put on his head a sheet of byblus spread out wide for a diadem, clothed the rest of his body with a rug for a royal robe. . . . Then from the multitudes standing round him there rang out a tremendous shout hailing him as Marin, which is said to be the name for 'lord' in Syria" [see 1 Cor. 16:22: *Mara Na Tha;* Lord, Please Come!] (*Philo, Flaccus [In Flaccum],* IX, 6:36–40, trans. F. H. Colson [Cambridge: Harvard University Press, 1954], p. 323).

2

Human Attempts at
Understanding Theography

Introduction

In his linguistic-philologic study, Geza Vermes disarms us with the obvious: ". . . the most alarming element of the Christian story [to the Church through the centuries] was the incomprehensible fiasco of an essentially Jewish religious movement among the Jewish people themselves."[1] How explain that, save for the visionary few, an entire nation could be so unimpressed by a Galilaean messenger with his "good news"? The response to this query may be found in the antiquity of the message. As Mircea Eliade puts it, the identification of the hero with an archetype equips him with a mythical biography.[2]

Can we imagine for a time that there are *no* gospel writings and, if we can shed the cultural prepossessions induced by their tradition, what sources could be identified that would yield a clue concerning some core beliefs that have acquired widespread diffusion? Could that phenomenon of diffusion be accounted for?

Savior Gods

Circa 3000 years *before the common era,* there was a savior born of a virgin mother, Innana (later to become Ishtar), and his Babylonian name—whence he originated—was Tammuz (Son of Life). By god-like transmigration, his name was attached to a cave in the townlet of Beyt Leḥem (Bethlehem) in Kenaan (Canaan). Known as the Cave of Tammuz, it became a fabled cultic center of a redeemer-god of vegetation, the embodiment of the reconstitutive energy of nature. Women used to weep for him when he died every year, and their lamentations were supposed to aid sympathetically in his annual rebirth. Ezekiel 8:14 tells of these women wailing for Tammuz. In the myth of the "Descent of Ishtar to the Nether World," Tammuz was washed with pure water and anointed with sweet oil as the wailers intoned: "May the dead rise and smell the incense."[3] Tammuz had his counterpart in other lands: in Syria, the Son of Life imported from Akkad was known as Adon or Adonis; in Phrygia, he was called Attis; in Egypt, Serapis or Osiris. The Greek version of the annual disappearance and reappearance of Tammuz was portrayed in the well-known story of Adonis and Aphrodite. After the institutionalization of Christianity, Christians and pagans alike were struck by the similarity between their respective deities, each one claiming the other as counterfeit. Jerome, who lived in Bethelehem (Beyt Leḥem) from 386 until his death in 420 C.E., wrote: "Even my own Bethelehem . . . was overshadowed by a grove of Tammuz, that is of Adonis; and in the very cave where the infant Christ had uttered his earliest cry lamentation was made for the paramour of Venus." (See the comment by Frazer.[4])

In the fourth century C.E., Bishop Eusebius, the preeminent Church historian, argued that the apparent junior position of Jesus was due to the wiles of the devil who inverted the usual order of nature, while Eliade would remind us that "an object or an act becomes real only insofar as it imitates or repeats an archetype. Thus reality is acquired solely through repetition or participation. . . ."[5] The words of the respected archaeologist William F. Albright are somewhat unusual as theoretical explanation. As he assessed the claims of rival savior gods—Tammuz, Osiris, Adonis, Attis— he concluded that they are but superficial resemblances to Jesus, that their appeal was "as different as light from darkness," because "these aspects of paganism [were as the church fathers declared] part of the divine preparation for Christianity."[6]

One characteristic that all savior gods possessed was that their births were the result of a divine manifestation. Indeed, in the early dawn of human history, *all* births were viewed as a deep-seated mystery; the diffusion of knowledge of the sexual function and its relationship to procreation came slowly. If it is found difficult to believe that humans lacked such basic knowledge, one need but recall how long it took for the race to employ the wheel or to work with metals. Even when they *saw* the application of wheels by European settlers, the American Indians dragged their belongings from an old site to a new one. Seeing alone does not confer theoretical understanding. The mystery of children was at first associated with some secret power that women alone possessed: the power of regeneration of life from within. Hence, the first supreme deities were female. In another stage of human development, all births were originally virginal, that is, the result of visitations by a god or gods to women, the visitation representing a divine gift to them. Later, that gift, particularly the first-born, was reclaimed by the gods since it was an emanation from them in the first place, and the idea of sacrificial offerings appeared. That heroes such as Sargon, Romulus, Cyrus, and Alexander the Great were divine figures, representing a blessing from the gods, can be understood within the theory that all births were a supernatural phenomenon, absent a natural theory as explanation. Generally, there is little trouble in comprehending that animal sexuality is expressed through instinctual behavior without cognitive understanding, yet we are given to wonder that humans once lacked the means adequately to comprehend and describe a natural function. Theoretical knowledge of sexual congress as a procreative force evolved rather than erupted, and its development may actually run parallel with those understandings that we usually connect with expressions of religion.

The Tradition of Emperor Worship

"The birthday of God has brought to the world glad tidings. . . . From his birthday, a new era begins." In speaking thus of Augustus Caesar, the emperor was not apotheosized; he *was* already divine, in keeping with Eastern (particularly Egyptian) traditions which held that God was incarnated in man. The resolution on deification honors adopted in 9 B.C.E. by a provincial assembly in Asia Minor follows:

> Whereas the Providence which has guided our whole existence . . . has brought our life to the peak of perfection in giving to us Augustus Caesar whom it (Providence) filled with virtue (Aretē) for the welfare of mankind, and who, being sent to us and to our descendants as a savior (sōtēr), has put an end to war and has set all things in order; and whereas having become visible (Phaneis, i.e., now that a God has become visible), Caesar has fulfilled the hopes of all earlier times . . . and whereas, finally, that the birthday of the God (viz. Caesar Augustus) has been for the whole world the beginning of the gospel (euangelion) concerning him, (therefore, let all reckon a new era beginning from the date of his birth, and let his birthday mark the beginning of the new year).[7]

In later centuries, assemblies came to make all sorts of declarations and observations about the way things "should" be; however, like the above, they were couched in phraseology that purported to describe conditions in the world empirically. Even though it is recognized as a self-centered, vainglorious human tendency, such recognition has little effect on the tendency itself. As may be seen from the foregoing declaration, the dominant thoughts of the time stand revealed. Practices based on such a system of thought were expressed in divine titles—a *commonplace* among rulers, military leaders, philosophers, literati, and other notables such as Epicurus (340–270 B.C.E.). Claims to divinity, then, need to be comprehended as expressive of a very old tradition, rather than something unique and one-of-its-kind.

A First-Century Holy Man Rival

The traditions of savior gods and emperor worship provide a glimpse into the style of thought of the early centuries of the common era. An outstanding exemplar of prevailing thought-patterns of the Roman-Greek world of the first century C.E. was the figure of Apollonius of Tyana. This historical personage from Cappadocia in Asia Minor, born in 2 B.C.E., became a nonagenarian, living through the reigns of nine Roman emperors, and dying ca. 98 C.E. (The tally of the emperors excludes the year 69 C.E. when four emperors reigned simultaneously.)

The birth of Apollonius occurred amid portents and heavenly apparitions, so we are told. As a youth, he preaches in the Temple of Zeus to the amazement of the populace. He revives a maiden from death in Rome and he knows languages without learning them. His portrait is that of a miracle worker and wandering teacher who sets forth simple words in pithy proverbs, highly suggestive of more than one meaning. Apollonius is an example of modest living, eating no animal flesh and condemning the sacrificial system while praising pure justice and exhorting his followers to live lives of self-denial. In principle, the stories about him were undifferentiable from those told of other holy figures such as Pythagoras, Buddha, Elijah (Eli-yahu), John the Baptist, and Jesus the Nazirite. These included an enormous following who ascribed to him a variety of unusual characteristics, visions of occurrences later to be corroborated, vanishing suddenly, cure of the sick by driving out demons, raising the dead, and personal resurrection and ascension to heaven.

According to a later biographer of the third century C.E., in his trial for sedition before the Roman Emperor Domitian, Apollonius was asked whether he was a god. In the testimony of the biographer, Apollonius also predicted the murder of Domitian and saw it in a vision from afar, *as* it was occurring. Apart from these marvels and the hagiologic biography written by Philostratus (ca. 170–244 C.E.) upon commission by the wife of Emperor Septimus Severus (ca. 217 C.E.), there are, in fact, some extant writings by Apollonius himself: a treatise on sacrifices and a biography of Pythagoras. In one of his extant letters, *Epistle XI of Apollonius to the Chief Councillors of Caesarea,* he wrote: "Men's first need is of gods for everything and above everything. . . ."[8]

The noted Edward Gibbon, who observed that Apollonius was born about the same time as Jesus the Nazirite, said that his life was spoken of in so fabulous a manner by his fanatic disciples that we can't discern whether he was a sage or an impostor. No less than Saint Augustine considered Apollonius higher than Zeus in the pagan hierarchy, but declared that it was absurd to rank him above Jesus. Indeed, Apollonius was stigmatized by church fathers Origen and Eusebius as devil-inspired and as proof of anti-Christian teaching through mockery. There is something strange in this charge. Tyana, in Cappadocia, was culturally similar to the site of Paul's ministry and in proximity to Paul's hometown of Tarsus. If Philostratus was guilty of writing an anti-Christian tract in his biography of Apollonius, we might expect some anti-Christian sentiment being expressed by the teacher from Tyana. Yet, if silence is any indication, none is apparent, while such is ascribed to him after the publication of his *Life* in 220 C.E. by Philostratus. Eusebius lays great stress on the lack of a pedigree by Apollonius; in contrast Jesus the Nazirite *had* a pedigree, i.e., he was "the only man of whom it was prophesied, thanks to their divine inspiration by Hebrew sages who lived far back thousands of years ago, that he [a Savior] should once come among mankind. . . ."[9] What Eusebius (living in the fourth century C.E.) conceives of as evidence can more readily be seen as a *claim* as well as official doctrine. Christianity having become the state religion in the fourth century C.E., it is not surprising that Apollonius disappeared from historical view as an unknown, the act of suppression being deemed meritorious.

Evidence from Sources Outside Gospel Writings

There are claims to only two sources outside gospel writings: the *Testimonium Flavianum,* a disputed excerpt from Josephus (93 C.E.), and a single passage in Tacitus's *Annals* (ca. 117 C.E.). Each of these will be presented as a distinct unit.

Josephus

Since Josephus became important to the Roman war effort in Judaea (65–73 C.E.) and then subsequently to Church historians, some prefatory remarks concerning his life are appropriate.

Joseph ben Matthias, also known as Flavius Josephus, was born of a priestly family in Jerusalem in 37 C.E. In his autobiography, he relates that he joined the Pharisee political party at age nineteen and remained within it throughout his life. In light of what has been attributed to him, this assertion of his is of extreme importance. At age twenty-nine, Josephus became an army commander in Galilee in the national struggle against Roman rule, which ended in the surrender of the entire area to Roman arms in 67 C.E. In the company of the Roman army commander, Titus, he witnessed the destruction of Jerusalem in 70–71 C.E. Given a pension by the Flavian Emperors Vespasian and Titus, Josephus retired in Rome with a commission to write *The Wars of the Jews,* followed by the mammoth history, *The Antiquities of the Jews.* These efforts occupied the last twenty-five years of his life, his death occurring ca. 102 C.E.

It is noteworthy that the very first Jewish book to be published in the United States of America was that of Josephus! It is also significant that in the last half-century alone, there have been several thousand articles and books on Josephus, whereas in none of the sixty-three voluminous tractates of the Talmud, compiled over a period of at least six centuries, is there so much as a mention of his name! The quantity of attention paid to Josephus is in no small measure due to the Christian Church, since he is absolutely indispensable to the claimed authentication of gospel testimonies *as historiography.* This may be seen in the so-called Christ passage in *The Antiquities of the Jews,* XVIII, 3:3. What is noteworthy about the passage is that between the fourth to the sixteenth centuries—the period of Church supremacy—the passage remained undisputed. However, since the sixteenth century, it has been the focus of a torrential outpouring of ink. The extended quotation from Book XVIII, 3:3, as given in Emil Schürer, follows:

> Now there was about this time, Jesus, a wise man, if it be lawful to call him a man, for he was a doer of wonderful works—a teacher of such men as receive the truth with pleasure. He drew over to him both many of the Jews and many of the Gentiles. He was the Christ; and when Pilate, at the suggestion of the principal men amongst us, had condemned him to the cross, those that loved him at the first did not forsake him, for he appeared to them alive again the third day, as the divine prophets had foretold these and ten thousand other wonderful things concerning him; and the tribe of Christians so named from him are not extinct at this day.[10]

Since the sixteenth century, the authenticity of this passage has been subjected to searching scrutiny by generations of scholars, and most hold that it is spurious. Some have analyzed it from fine points of technical language use while others focus on the content of what is said. The latter focus is adopted here since the content is manifestly self-indicting. It is not too difficult to view the entire passage as foreign to the pen of Josephus, inasmuch as the designation *Christians* fairly "leaps out" at once, as a clear retrojection. At this point in the first century, Josephus did not know the term "Christian" nor did the Romans. In the first century C.E., "outsiders" referred to the faith community (later called Christian) as Galileans or as Natzoreans (Nazarenes), while among themselves, within the faith community, they called each other Brethren, Believers, or even Saints. A fairly common judgment concerning the nomen "Christian" has it that it was first coined at Antioch in Syria by the external populace and then employed by Bishop Ignatius (ca. 110 C.E.). This datum alone is sufficient to cast doubt on the authorship of the above passage.

Further support comes from a most unlikely source: the monumental work of historian Bishop Eusebius of Caesarea (264–340 C.E.). In his *Ecclesiastical History* (*H. E.*) II, 17:1–24, he refers to the famous Alexandrian Jewish leader Philo (Philon, 20 B.C.E.–50 C.E.). Eusebius claims that according to tradition, Philo met Peter while in Rome during the reign of Emperor Claudius (41–54 C.E.), and that in one of his written works (*On Suppliants*) Philo described the ascetic life of an early confraternity then called *Therapeutae* (Healers), "for as yet the name *Christians* had not spread everywhere." In citing Philo's description of this group of ascetics whom he called *Therapeutae,* Eusebius concludes: "It seems to me that these words of Philo are a clear and undeniable reference to the followers of our doctrine."[11] With these indirect statements, Eusebius unwittingly offers confirmation that no group *before* 50 C.E. (the date of Philo's death) could conceivably have been known by the name "Christian"! On another point, Eusebius is mistaken in thinking that the Alexandrian confraternity, Therapeutae, was an "early Christian" brotherhood.

If further evidence were required that the term "Christian" was unknown to Josephus in the first century, it comes from the pen of the Roman Stoic philosopher, Epictetus (50?–126? C.E.). He, along with other philosophers, was banished from Rome by the Emperor Domitian in 89 C.E., yet Epictetus's writings were a profound influence on the great Stoic Emperor Marcus Aurelius (161–180 C.E.). In his *Discourses,* Epictetus used two different terms for the faith community later to be known as "Christian." In one reference, *Discourses,* Book II, chapter 9, he calls the group *Jews* and in *Discourses,* Book IV, chapter 7, he entitles the "group" *Galilaeans:*

> He is not a Jew, he is only acting the part. But when he adopts the attitude of mind of the man who has been baptized and has made his

choice, then he both is a Jew in fact and is also called one. So we also are but counterfeit "baptists," Jews in name only, but really something else.[12]

One reason why some might find the above passage confusing is that of cultural prepossession: the built-in tendency to anachronize our categories, retrojecting them into an age where they did not yet exist. It may be observed that Epictetus was a younger contemporary of Josephus, and it seems clear that this celebrated first-century author knew only about a community called Jews or Galilaeans. That "Christians" were later to be confused with Jews is not too surprising since religiously focused distinctions were not apparent to the Romans.

In his savage punishment of "the incendiaries" of Rome in 64 C.E., the Emperor Nero knew of no distinctions between Jewish messianists, as may be seen in the next section on Tacitus. Indeed, it was more often as Jews that messianists would suffer. For instance, in 70 C.E. Emperor Vespasian had ordered a search for all descendants of the House of David, but once imprisoned, they were later released.[13] His son, Domitian, eleven years later ordered the execution of any remaining descendants of the royal house. Later, in the reign of Emperor Trajan (98–117 C.E.), the same descendants were again arrested.[14] What significance may be found in data of this sort? The Messiah (Meshiaḥ) had to come from the seed of David.

It was only after the reign of Emperor Nerva (96–98 C.E.) that the *two* groups of Messianists—those who looked to the past and those who looked to the future—came to be differentiated in Roman eyes. There is physical evidence for this conclusion. After the destruction of the Temple in Jerusalem in 70 C.E., the Emperor Vespasian had established the *Fiscus Judaicus*[15]; a half-shekel capitation tax was to be paid annually in lieu of the former Temple tax that Jews had voluntarily assessed themselves. Like the Temple tax, it was imposed on all Jews residing anywhere within the Roman Empire, a sizable number of men and women from ages three to sixty-two. In Emperor Nerva's reign, he issued a special commemorative coin: *Fisci judaici calumnia sublata* (On the removal of the shameful [extortion of the] Jewish fiscal tax), wherein fiscal obligation rested only on *professing* Jews and *not* on renegade Jews or slaves of Jews (as under the previous emperor, Domitian, 81–96 C.E.[16]). This was indirect recognition of the schism and severance of ties between Jews and Galilaeans or Natzoreans. Again, it seems more than clear that the phrase "tribe of Christians" appearing in the passage in Josephus XVIII is a much later addendum. One authority on Josephus indulges in complex analysis of the "colour" of Josephus's words and his commonly used phrases; it becomes an intense struggle, with might and main, to capture *him* as the prize. And what a prize—an independent witness! What is absolutely crucial is whether the designation "Christian" was knowable to Josephus at the time of his composition of *Antiquities;* the rest seems peripheral and inconsequential.[17]

What also should be obvious is that gospel testimonies were not available to Josephus, who was composing his huge opus over a score of years from 73 to 93 C.E. No gospel writing appeared before the fateful date of the destruction of Jerusalem in 70 C.E. In the earliest gospel testimony, that attributed to Mark, in 13:1–4 he speaks of the disaster in Jerusalem about to overtake the city. Yet, there is no external evidence of Mark until the second century; neither of the earliest apostolic fathers (those who knew the apostles themselves) Bishop Ignatius (d. 117 C.E.) nor Polycarp (70–155 C.E.) show any knowledge of Mark. (It may also be remembered that the oldest physical evidence—an extant manuscript of the gospel writings—dates from the fourth century C.E.) It is very puzzling indeed to find in the "Christ Passage" in Book XVIII a division of responsibility for the death of Jesus between Pilate and Jews—a clear indication of acquaintance with gospel writings! How can this be explained?

It is tempting to ascribe authorship of the Christ passage in Josephus to Eusebius, as does Solomon Zeitlin in *The Rise and Fall of the Judean State.*[18] What apparently convinces Zeitlin to make the charge of "artistic forgery" and to lay the interpolation at the door of Eusebius is that the Christ passage was never cited by a single church father prior to the fourth century C.E., that is, prior to the Council of Nicea in 325 C.E. Even as late as the ninth century, the passage was not to be found in the famous library at Constantinople. The patriarch of the Great Church, Bishop Photius, had carefully studied and annotated three hundred "ancient" works in the famed Biblioteca; his copy of Josephus contained no such phrase as "He was the Christ."[19] It seems most unlikely that such a declaration or pronouncement, had it conceivably been made by Josephus, would not have evoked more explanatory detail from a writer whose dominant characteristic was attention to the minute. Moreover, Alexandrian church father Origen (185–254 C.E.), whose influence on Eusebius was profound, explicitly asserts that Josephus did *not* believe that Jesus was the Messiah. It is also peculiar that Origen himself ignores the Christ passage even as he comments upon the James passage (*Antiquities,* Book XX:9). It seems obvious that such a passage did not exist in his copy of the Josephus manuscript, as this passage from Origen's *Commentary on Matthew* X.17 indicates:

> Josephus . . . desirous of setting forth the reason for which the people [of Judaea] experienced such suffering that even the temple was destroyed, stated that these things happened to them in accordance with the wrath

of God because of what they ventured to do to James the brother of
Jesus the so-called Christ. [sic!] What is marvellous is that although
Josephus did not accept our Jesus as Christ, he nonetheless ascribed
such righteousness to James: he says that the people supposed that they
suffered these things on account of James.[20]

Let it be noted that the James passage (Josephus, *Antiquities* XX:9)
referred to in the writings of church father Origen (*Contra Celsum* I:47)
is the subject of much confusion and doubt. Was *this* passage penned
by Josephus or is it a reinterpreted version of him? Many have tried to
disentangle the original from the revised version, attributed by some to
Origen himself. One of the very first to try was the celebrated Church
historian, learned Bishop Eusebius of Caesarea (264–340 C.E.).

Eusebius quotes Hegesippus at length, although from fragments, on
the death of "James the brother of the Lord."[21] Hegesippus (ca. 120–180
C.E.) was an ardent Jewish convert to Christianity who resided in Rome
from 155 C.E. on. Eusebius tells us that he "arranged the narrative chrono-
logically" since Hegesippus was no historian and was occupied with matters
of orthodoxy and heresy, not historical fact. Eusebius himself was guided
by theological concerns on the enemies of God![22] One has also to deal
with Origen's account and interpretation of Josephus, and his preoccupation with Christian theodicy: the reasons for the fall of Jerusalem. It
is surprising that Eusebius was able to extricate himself from the thicket
of conflicting accounts, but as he describes himself as "anthologizing the
words of the ancient writers as from spiritual meadows," perhaps the dis-
tilled product was his own—a James reference of pious passion—to
transform a society of thought.[23]

Among the esteemed scholars who have questioned the authenticity
of the Christ passage in *Antiquities* XVIII was the noted Emil Schürer.
In 1886 he wrote: "We may surely be at least unanimous as to this, that
the words, as we have them now, were not written by Josephus. Whatever
may be advanced in their favor does not amount to much in comparison
with the unquestionable indications of spuriousness."[24] Schürer disputes
not only the Christ passage, but also the James passage (*Antiq.* XX.9)
with its reference to the brother of Jesus, which occupied Hegesippus,
Origen, and Eusebius at great lengths. He regards this, too, as interpolation by Christian hands during the period of church father Origen, i.e.,
185–255 C.E.

Although the dominant scholarship judges the so-called testimony of
a non-Christian source as inauthentic and spurious, the passages can also
be understood as being within the tradition of natural expansiveness, as
the process has been described heretofore in earlier pages: creative gap-

filling and amplification on God's revelations that were faith-inspired commentary, in order to make the account more and more complete. This is hardly conceived as forgery or falsification; on the contrary, it is expatiation on inspiration. Convinced by burning zeal that one was Christ-possessed, what could be more courageous than to expand and expound on his manifest presence. Hegesippus, Origen, and Eusebius might have reasoned as follows: "Surely, Josephus must have known of Christ and appreciated his immanent entry into the world of men. It remains only to complete what Josephus already had in mind." However, with Josephus it could not be said "Let the Scriptures Be Fulfilled," since he wrote as historian, not as prophetic oracle. As an astute writer has observed: "The Christian interpolator of Josephus undoubtedly thought he was helping history to confirm faith. All he succeeded in doing was to remove any independent value from the testimony of Josephus."[25]

Tacitus

Attention is now focused on the second of the sources external to gospel writings used as corroborative evidence, a passage in Tacitus's *Annals,* written ca. 117–123 C.E.[26] The outstanding authority Ronald Syme, professor of Ancient History at Oxford, wrote: "The historian Tacitus, carefully noting an incident at Rome in the sequel of the great conflagration under Nero, registers the origin of the name 'Christian' with documentary precision."[27] As will be demonstrated, the claim of "documentary precision" is but tendentious prepossession and becomes the artful inscribing of error into immortality. However, first to the passage from *The Annals* XLIV, 1–8:

> But neither human help, nor imperial munificence, nor all the modes of placating Heaven, could stifle scandal or dispel the belief that the fire had taken place by order. Therefore, to scotch the rumour, Nero substituted as culprits and punished with the utmost refinements of cruelty, a class of men loathed for their vices, whom the crowd styled Christians. Christus, the founder of the name, had undergone the death penalty in the reign of Tiberius by sentence of the procurator Pontius Pilate, and the pernicious superstition was checked for a moment, only to break out once more, not merely in Judaea, the home of the disease, but in the capital itself, where all things horrible or shameful in the world collect and find a vogue. First, then, the confessed members of the sect were arrested; next, on their disclosures, vast numbers were convicted, not so much on the count of arson as for hatred of the human race.[28]

It is to be observed that Tacitus wrote of the great fire of Rome (64 C.E.) at a distance in excess of fifty years. There were copious Roman records for this notable event, but what records did Tacitus use in speaking of "Christians"? Did he use Josephus? Certainly that history was available to him. His mentioning of *apparently* distinct events in the above passage should not be misconstrued: the fire in Rome in 64 C.E. and the outbreak of revolt in Judaea (65 C.E.), "the home of the disease." The connector between these two events is "the founder of the name" [nomen christianum] who is sentenced by the procurator. A second connector links Jesus and Pilate, but what is Tacitus's *source* for all this?

Tacitus does *not* derive his information from Roman records, since there are *no* Roman records of such a death penalty being imposed on "the founder of the name." Despite the claim of Professor Syme of "documentary precision," the evidence points just to the contrary! Tacitus cannot be considered *independent* testimony, inasmuch as he is merely repeating what he has heard about a then-nascent movement. How can we know this? Had Tacitus worked from archives, he would have become aware that Pontius Pilate was *not* a procurator. The title recorded by Tacitus, ca. 120 C.E., remained fixed until the year 1961, affecting accounts about the Roman fire from the second century to the twentieth. For it was only from the time of Emperor Claudius (41–54 C.E.) that provincial governors bore the title "Procurator Augustii," and only with regard to Judaea and not Galilee, which was governed by local tetrarchs from the House of Herod. From the year 6 C.E. to 41 C.E., prefects were "in charge of" Judaea, which means that they did *not* have ultimate authority, but were responsible directly to the emperor and his legate in Syria, Judaea not being considered either a sovereign or autonomous unit or even geographically distinct.

In 1961 an inscription found at Caesarea, Israel, recording the dedication of a building in honor of Emperor Tiberius, gives Pilate's title as praefectus of Judaea. (A photograph of the building showing Pilate's title may be seen in Arnold Toynbee's *The Crucible of Christianity*.[29]) Indeed, the tablet itself is on display at Caesarea as part of a tourist attraction. Tour guides continue to refer to Pontius Pilate as a procurator nonetheless, even when the title *Praefectus* is pointed out to them. Such was the experience of this writer on a visit to Caesarea in the summer of 1993. Outright denial then yields to the insignificance of "what's the difference?" It is indeed difficult to alter a comfortable thought pattern. The significance is that this simple, obscure fact calls into question Tacitus's "testimony" regarding an execution of which he knows nothing. Rather than consulting records, he uses a title (procurator) current in *his* lifetime and retrojects it to the years from 29 to 33 C.E., including the hearsay, connecting the "procurator" with Jesus. How trustworthy could the "independent" testimony of an eminent historian be who gave Abraham Lincoln the title of king or prime minister? Similarly, Tacitus's use of the descriptive title *Christus* as if it were a proper name while not citing the actual name of the accused *at best* demonstrates careless anachronism; at worst, a suspicion of interpolation is aroused. Such critical errors in a professional historian have been copied for centuries by learned scholars. The title Christus was not in use in 64 C.E. as a name; rather, it was expression of a messianic idea or hope. Thus, as Lactantius (ca. 313 C.E.) writes: "For Christ is not His proper name but the name of power and dominion: this, indeed, the Jews name their kings [meshiaḥ adonai]."[30]

John Jackson, translator of the passage in *Annals* XLIV, makes a very revealing observation: the phrase "hatred of the human race" was a common description of Jews, "Jewish 'misanthropy'—which was proverbial—may have partly suggested the charge [of hatred]. . . ."[31] This serious indictment of a whole people raises the very important question of the identity of the group whom Nero charged with arson and upon whom he inflicted such devilish reprisals. It is noteworthy that the fire first broke out in the Jewish Quarter of Rome, where eight thousand Jewish residents lived. Lacking nomenclature that was developed and refined much later, Romans had no way of speaking about apocalyptists and messianists except as fanatical Jews. (See below on the expulsion of Jews from Rome by Emperor Claudius in 54 C.E.) As previously indicated, the *Fiscus Judaicus* of 96–98 C.E. marks the official note of Roman distinction between Jews who looked forward to a messiah (meshiaḥ) and those who thought that he had already arrived. By the time of Emperors Trajan and Hadrian (117–118 C.E.), the sect, Christians, was noted in Trajan's letter to his governor, Pliny, but this does not gainsay the identity of those accused of arson in 64 C.E.

The great historian of Rome, Edward Gibbon, spends a great part of chapter 16 in the *Decline and Fall of the Roman Empire* on the fire of 64 C.E. The celebrated author delivers himself of a fierce denunciation and racial assault on Jews, so he can hardly be considered an apologist. He insists upon distinguishing the Galilaean followers of Jesus of Nazareth from the radical nationalist party of Galilaeans (also known as Zealots) who were followers of Judas the Gaulonite (the territory of Golan).

> The former [Galilaean followers of Jesus] were the friends, the latter [Galilaean followers of Judas] were the enemies of human kind. How natural was it for Tacitus, in the time of Hadrian, to appropriate to the Christians the guilt and sufferings which he might, with far greater truth and justice, have attributed to a sect whose odious memory was almost extinguished.[32]

Presumably, Gibbon is here referring to the mass deportation, displacement, and dispersal of Jews by Hadrian before (as well as after) the ill-fated Bar Kokhba Rebellion in 135 C.E. Here, from a most unlikely and unexpected quarter, comes the notion that the term "Christian" was not known—much less employed—in 64 C.E.; that on the contrary, Galilaean groups were easily confounded, the friends of the human race and the enemies of humanity, i.e., Jews. In Gibbon's judgment, Tacitus was entirely too loose in his identification of the accursed arsonists in Rome, since neither he nor Nero, in 64 C.E., knew the difference between Galilaeans of the Jesus or Judas variety.

If we return now to the "connectors" of Tacitus between the fire in Rome and the revolt in Judaea of 65/66, there could not have been too much love between Jews and Romans in 64 C.E. Josephus describes the air of tense and charged apocalypticism that prevailed in the first half of the first century, and he condemns apocalyptists as deceivers who foster revolution. As the following selection makes clear, Josephus regarded apocalyptists as charlatans and their followers as deluded: "Deceivers and impostors under the pretense of divine inspiration fostering revolutionary changes, they persuaded the multitude to act like madmen and led them out into the desert under the belief that God would give them tokens of deliverance."

Josephus goes on to refer to the "prophet" Theudas (ca. 45 C.E.), who promised to divide the waters of the Jordan River, and also to an Egyptian-Jewish messiah who in 52–54 C.E. brought thirty thousand Jerusalemites to the Mount of Olives declaring "that he would show from hence how, at his command, the walls of Jerusalem would fall down."[33] Roman soldiers speedily and bloodily suppressed both commotions. It suffices to say that almost anyone in this period of chiliastic fervor and heightened expectancy could command a following. (It is important to note that the above material from *Antiquities* XX is in stark contrast with the claimed Christ passage of Book XVIII 3.3; it is most unlikely that the same author could have written both.)

Given the atmosphere of chiliasm within the Roman Empire described by Josephus, it is not surprising to find that the emperor Claudius, generally kindly disposed toward his Jewish subjects, banished them from Rome in 54 C.E. because, at the "instigation of chrestos" ("*impulsore chresto*"), they created constant unrest. This phrase from Suetonius was published in 120 or 121 C.E.[34] Do we have here a mere terminological problem of mispronunciation? Hardly! "Since the Jews constantly made disturbances at the instigation of chrestos, he [Claudius] expelled them from Rome."[35] (It may be noted that the expulsion was only temporary.)

The Greek term *chrestos,* meaning "good" or "worthy," would have been comprehensible to the Greeks or Romans, whereas *meshiaḥ* or "anointed one"—*christos*—would have been unintelligible. Furthermore, why would Jews and not Christians in 54 C.E. be involved with *chrestos,* presumably a Gnostic designation for *logos,* goodness or kindness? Here is indirect proof from 121 C.E. that the name "Christians" was not known in 54 C.E.

Several important Christian writers point out that *Chrestos* was confused with *Christus* as Jehovah might substitute for YHVH and Joshua for Yoshua. But the latter are differences in sound due to a complete change in language; they are not *errors* of pronunciation within a similar linguistic system. Tacitus's manuscript was read by Harnack as "Chrestianos apellabat," and he says the mob called them "blunderingly" "Chrestians," but that "this was subsequently corrected."[36] As may be seen in Justin (ca. 150 C.E.) the term *chrestian* is not a "blunder" at all! Justin declares: "For we are accused of being Christians, yet to hate what is *excellent* [chrestian] [*sic,* emphasis and translation in the original] is unjust."[37]

The idea of slipshod pronunciation is reinforced and then negated in Tertullian, writing in 197-198 C.E. He says that "Christian" was mispronounced as "chrestian" by Roman magistrates. However, he also points out that it was because *chrestos* ("sweetness" or "kindness") was more familiar and obvious to them (though rarely used as a name) than *Christos,* a translation of a word foreign to them.[38] Lactantius (313 C.E.) refers to an "error of ignorance"—a clear projection of his belief on to others who do not share the belief.[39] There is no error at all! The earlier term *chrestos* was not a mistaken pronunciation for *christus,* but rather the reverse; the later term entered the language as a title and *it* became confounded with the earlier term, not the reverse as Tertullian and Lactantius suggest. (See Justin's *Apology,* note 37.)

The stress on the distinction between the two terms is a necessary if trying one. Suetonius, writing in 121, tells us of a Jewish community in Rome creating disturbances in 54 C.E. and he does not make an error in names at all! Tacitus, writing in the same time period, takes the *nomen christianum* of *his* day—"Christus the founder of the name"—and retrojects it to the period of Nero's reign. In so inscribing error, he damages the record for centuries[40] and is responsible for diffusing misinformation whose damage cannot even be estimated. What emerges from the tangle and thicket is that, in the events of 64 C.E. as reported by Tacitus, the designation "Christian" was unknown currency. While in the New Testament, *Acts of the Apostles* 26:28 asserts that the name "Christian" arose in the home of the first Gentile church, the term itself was presumably being used by the Antiochene Father Ignatius, ca. 110-115 C.E.[41] Although we do not know when *Acts of the Apostles* was written, it certainly did not antedate composition of *The Gospel According to Luke* (ca. 125). What seems certain is that Tacitus, lacking warrant for his assertions and with no official Roman record to rely on, cannot be portrayed as providing independent testimony for the existence of a "Christian" community in Rome in 64 C.E., the term "Christian" appearing no earlier than the second decade of the second century.

Sources of Jesus' Biography

Free-floating material does not disappear. It washes up here and, much later, there. Such is the proto-history of the idea of salvation (*yeshua*). Lactantius (250/60–317 C.E.) tells us that

> The Greeks called Josue [Yoshua] "Jesus" for the two names are the same in Hebrew. The meaning is "savior." It was not without significance. Moses by his law could only bring the people within sight of the promised inheritance but our savior, Jesus (prefigured by Josue), was to bring us into it.[42]

Not only does Lactantius aver that Yoshua of the fourteenth precentury prefigures Jesus, he supplements the claim of prefiguring with a theory of supersession: the old testament is to be replaced by the new.

The basis for Lactantius may be found in Exodus 23:20,21:

> I am sending a messenger [some translate *malakh* as "angel"] before you, to guard you on the way and to bring you to the place which I have made ready. Pay heed to him and obey him. Do not defy him for he will not pardon your offenses, since my Name is in him [i.e., Yeho— or Yo—shua].

Verse 23:23 identifies this individual: "When my messenger goes before you and brings you to the A[E]morite, the Hittite, the Perizzite, Kenaanite, the Hivvite, and the J[Y]ebusite, and I annihilate them, you shall not bow down to their gods in worship." A similar sentence with identical names of nations appears in Joshua (Yehoshua) 3:19. The promise is made that under the leadership of this messenger (angel), certain nations resident in Kenaan would be conquered. It seems that Exodus 23:21 specifies that only one who has the name Yeho or Yo can lead Israel to triumph. Yehoshua thus appears to be a god-figure, perhaps an ancient deity, later reduced to human status. Indeed, all heroes at one time were either divine or took on divine proportions, as with Herakles and Samson. The divine proportion in Yehoshua is made explicit in his command to the sun and moon to "be still" in their courses (Joshua [Yehoshua] 10:12–13).

In apocalyptic writings known as Sibylline Oracles V, a post-Christian work, Jesus is identified with Yehoshua[43]:"Now a certain excellent man shall come again from heaven, who spread forth his hands upon the very fruitful tree, the best of the Hebrews, who once made the sun stand still, speaking with beauteous words and pure lips." A link is made explicit between a proto-Jesus (Yoshua) and a later one, reborn [a deliverer with a divine name]. The proto-Jesus is the son of Nōn (Nun), and with a very slight vowel change we have Nin. *Nun* is the name of a consonant in the Hebrew alphabet which translates as fish; *Nin* was a fish deity in the Assyrian pantheon, and one of the symbols of institutionalized Christianity was the fish, Tertullian calling Jesus (Yeshua) the divine fish. The well-known Greek formula for the word *Ichthys,* meaning fish, was *Iesous Christos Theou Yios Soter* (Jesus Christ God's Son Savior). This was probably nothing more than a mnemonic device, rather than the term being itself some sort of divine symbol. It is also interesting to note that the twelfth and last sign of the zodiac is the fish, thereby connected with the end of the world, known as the days of the messiah (mashiaḥ). The concept of meshiaḥ [anointed one] in early Jewish tradition, i.e., the period of the Judges, was that of a deliverer or *mōshia,* translated as "one who *helps* or *saves.*" Someone with a theophorous name like *Yeho*shua would be particularly impressive: a God-type with a God-name: "Yah helps" or "Ye is salvation." It may be noted that when the Judaeans returned from Babylonian exile in 520 B.C.E., the high priest was named Yehoshua. The prophet Zechariah in 3:8,9 speaks to him: "Listen, high priest, Yehoshua, you and your colleagues seated here before you, for they are an omen of good things to come: I shall now bring my servant the Branch (shoot). . . . In a single day I shall wipe away the guilt of this land." In this context, the name, Yehoshua, "God Saves," is notable, and the *Branch* (of David) is telling to Christian exegesis, as is the promise to "wipe away the guilt"; the expressions are of salient christological import.

Thus, it is easy to see why Justin believed that Yehoshua was a prototype of Jesus, why Origen identified the two, and why Lactantius wrote as he did. While the original form of the name given in the Book of Numbers is Hoshea ("helped"), it was altered by Moses to incorporate the reference to the deity (Numbers 13:16).[44]

It has also been suggested that Joshua (Yehoshua) may have been a mythological solar figure to whom were applied snatches of popular songs about unusual feats and marvellous accomplishments such as transpired in the Vale of Ayalon as referred to in Joshua (Yehoshua) 10:13,14: "Sun, Be Silent." In connection with this incident, two statements about the tomb of Joshua (Yehoshua) are most revealing. In Judges 2:9, Yehoshua's burial place is listed as Timnat Ḥeres (Portion of the Sun-god, in the hill country of Ephraim). In Joshua (Yehoshua) 19:50, the burial place is called Timnat Seraḥ (Portion of Licentiousness). SRḤ is the rendering of ḤRS backwards. Later interpretations held that the name Timnat Ḥeres was traced to an image of the sun that was placed over Joshua's (Yehoshua's) tomb. Were the consonants then deliberately transposed to Seraḥ to avoid the connection with sun worship? Evidently the place may have been the site of a sun cult, as a memorial to the one who uttered the epic "Be Silent" to the sun. (It may be noted, incidentally, that Jericho, destroyed by Joshua, was the center of a moon cult, as found in the translation of the name *Yeriḥo*. Was it near Yeriḥo that the sun overcame the moon in ancient myth?) The central question for us here is: Was this fourteenth-precentury figure a proto-divinity?

Important evidence on that question derives from the center of Joshua's (Yehoshua's) operations, the site called GLGL (Gilgal or Galgal), suggesting a circle. It was here that twelve stones were gathered as a memorial to the crossing of the River Jordan (Yarden) on dry land (Joshua/Yehoshua 4:4-7, 18-24), either a reenactment or prefiguring of the Israelite crossing of the Sea of Reeds as described in Exodus. Here also was the site of national circumcision (Joshua/Yehoshua 5:2-9). Verse 9 reports: "This day I have 'rolled' away the reproach of Egypt from off you." *Galgal* means "wheel" and, in popular usage, *gilgal* may suggest the idea of *rolling* stones. It seems clear that the stone circle or gilgal became, at once, a cultic center or religious sanctuary, as well as an amphictyonic center and military base of operations, however, its reputation soon became sullied (that is, in retrospective judgment) as may be noted in Judges 3:18,19 concerning Judge Ehud and the "carved stones (graven images) at Gilgal." By the time of the eighth century B.C.E. prophets, its practices were reprehended by them. Amos 4:4,5 declares: "Come to Beth El and transgress; to Gilgal and multiply your transgressions." Hoshea 4:15 declaims: "Though you play the harlot, Israel, yet let not Judah become guilty and come not unto Gilgal . . ." (also Hoshea 12:11). Such condemnations implicate Gilgal as a shrine for peculiar worship in the eyes of monotheistic prophets. What is most suggestive about the transposition of the letters of the recorded burial place of Yehoshua, from ḤRS (Ḥeres) to SRḤ (Seraḥ) is that it probably became a site of licentious worship forms, as the designation SRḤ itself announces. Tombs were notorious as centers of unusal practices around which a variety of cults and sects developed. For instance, the prophet Isaiah (Yesha-yahu, 65:4,5), condemns the swine-eaters and mouse-eaters who used to gather in gardens (66:17) for their eucharist-worship forms of these sacred animals. Indeed, the Judaic prohibition of the flesh of the swine probably had more to do with theology than with hygiene. Did the center of Joshua/Yoshua at Gilgal deteriorate in its cultic expression and practice? How else may the eighth-precentury condemnations be explained?

Additional evidence which points to the proto-divinity status of Joshua/ Yehoshua has to do with sacrificial executions. Joshua/Yehoshua 8:28,29 reads: "So Yoshua burnt Ai and made it a tel [mound] for ever . . . and the King of Ai [Place of Desolation] he hanged on a tree until the evening. . . ." At a place called Makkedah, there was a League of Five Kings in opposition to Yehoshua. As the narrative at 10:26 states: "And afterward, Yehoshua smote [pierced] them and put them to death, and hanged them on five trees and they were hanging upon the trees until the evening." The remainder of chapter 10 details the capture of six other city-states in the hill country of central Kenaan, and describes the fate of its kings, Yoshua being presented as the "dispatcher" of kings.[45]

In studying the history of religions, one becomes aware of the special status of the king: he is the embodiment of the nation's god. As the incarnation of divine life, that life has to be saved from the vessel in which it has been encased, that is, *detached* from it and transferred or "raised up." As the old representative of the god is killed and the divine spirit released in a new incarnation, the act of killing may also be seen as a necessary step to preservation, in a better form, of the spirit of the divine. The Roman emperor Vespasian expressed the idea on his deathbed in 79 C.E.: "I think I am going to become a god." Similarly, Emperor Caracalla (ca. 212 C.E.), who had his brother assassinated to remove a threat to his throne, approved of his brother's deification in these words: "Let him be a god so long as he is not alive."

A related theme is the idea of sacrificial death as a highly honorable one. Human sacrifice was, after all, the return of the gift of life to its giver. In this sense, the sacrificial victim *became* a god by the *act* of sacrifice, the sacrificial act being ascribed to the god as *both* slayer *and* slain. Osiris is the most notable example of a suffering and slain divinity; others are Dionysius, Adonis, and Attis. In Norse mythology, the chief god Odin was called Lord of the Gallows, or God of the Hanged, and is presented sitting under a gallows tree. He is both slayer and slain, having been sacrificed to himself: "I know that I hung on the windy tree for nine whole nights wounded with the spear dedicated to Odin, myself to myself."[46] (One may note the piercing with a spear and the telling ninth hour in the gospels narrative of crucifixion.)

The concatenation of ideas related to the nature of royal executions is a vast subject in itself. It is important to this work to the extent that a proto-Jesus (Yoshua/Yeshua) and a later one reborn are in some way connected with such practices, be their nature expiatory or sympathetic, or honorable and exemplary punishment. Whatever their nature, it is the rite itself which begets the narrative; it is not the narrative that produces the rite and it is a mistake to look to narrative for origins and historical fact. (See, for example, Frazer on the Roman Saturnalia.[47])

Further evidence on the question of the divinity status of Yoshua/ Yeshua may be seen in the ancient formula of exorcism: "I adjure you by Jesus, the god of the Hebrews. . . ." *Acts of the Apostles* 19:13,14 records the following: "Some itinerant Jewish exorcists tried their hand at using the name of the Lord Jesus on those possessed by evil spirits," adding "whom Paul proclaims." In Mark 9:38,39, the disciples say to Jesus: "Master, we saw someone driving out demons in your name and as he was not one of us, we tried to stop him. Jesus said, 'Do not stop him, for no one who performs a miracle in my name will be able the next moment to speak evil of me. He who is not against us is on our side." So, it is apparent that there *were* Yeshua sects—of independent origin— with power in the very name itself. What this points to is a popular religion around the figure of Yoshua, however discountenanced by such prophets as Amos and Hoshea, alongside the official Yahu worship. It seems that cults and confraternities at GLGL developed and crystallized around that figure or idea. Did the condemnations agains GLGL by Amos and Hoshea have to do with the practice of exorcism of demons? If a cult existed regarding a solar figure referred to as Yoshua/Yeshua around whom tales could accrete, all that was needed was to extend the story to his later sojourn on earth. In an age of belief, it would be but a short time and the story would be embellished and enhanced.

Marginal Cults and Confraternities

Unlike other national groups where religion is just one of many institutions that serve the nationhood, with Israel it was the nationhood that was made to serve the cult. Israel began as a religious community, a faith-creating unity among warring humanity. It lived in this form throughout its history, despite all disintegrating influences from the outside. It is not to be supposed that a monolithic structure was typical of Israel's history; despite monarchic attempts at centralization, free associations were much more the rule, with brotherhoods and confraternities existing for centuries, often the expression of a parallel popular religion. Such circles retained forgotten mysteries, archaic ideas and practices, seemingly bypassed by an official institution, for instance, human sacrifice or eucharistic meals with their partaking of divine substances. As carriers of traditions and fragments of localized practices that often ran counter to a mainstream institution, such associatons were frequently secret orders with ceremonies designed deliberately to segregate and insulate the association by divulging its mysteries only to the faithful. Among the minority groups in ancient Israel were a variety of prophetic associations: war prophets or, as more commonly known, judges; ecstatics; court prophets; free-speaking prophets; and prophets of doom. Some prophets were king-makers or king-breakers, a counterpower-center, often with popular support.

Another group, perhaps arising earlier than the various prophetic associations, was known as separated ones or Nazirenes. These were consecrated ecstatics, set apart by their ascetic abstinence and, in the spirit of YHVH, at holy war with indigenous fertility cults. Such "separated ones" were originally associated with a warrior-ascetic code, which consecrated them for battle. One allusion to them is found in Judges 5:2: "When men let their hair grow in Israel"; another is suggested in Deuteronomy 33:16,17, where the children of Joseph, accorded a double portion of land, apparently constitute the core of the armed forces. Military engagements themselves were viewed as sanctified rituals; as described in the Battle of Jericho (Yeriḥo), there was a stringent tabu against the private taking of booty (Yehoshua 7:1, 19-26). It may also be inferred that periodic abstinence from food and sex was part of the spiritual quarantine or warrior ascetic code. (See notes on 1 Samuel 14:24-30 and 14:43 and 2 Samuel 11:8, 11, 13.[48]) Perhaps the biggest tabu-breaker of the Nazirene Code was Samson, the ecstatic berserker who fell prey to his weakness for women. In later national development, Nazirenes were transformed toward a more pacific pattern of living, including mortification by vow and a ritually exemplary life of constraint (in keeping with the detailed regulations of Numbers 6:2-21).

The probable allies of, or successors to, the Nazirenes were the Rekhabites, another Yahu-ist sect. The founder Rekhav and his son *Yeho*-nadav proscribed the drinking of wine, which they held to be a divine commandment. According to Jeremiah (Yirmi-yahu) 35:2,12,18-19, we see their lifeway: a disdain for fixed settlement and agriculture and, with an idealization of semi-nomadic life, they are stockbreeders and tent dwellers who appear to have been part of the struggle against alcoholic orgiasticism as practised by the settled population. The Rekhabites first come to our attention in mid-ninth century B.C.E. when the prophet-king-breaker Elisha brought down the House of Omri, founder of Samaria, by whipping up this sect to stage a revolutionary coup; they spearhead the military operations in establishing Jehu (Yehu) as king and in his extirpation of the House of Omri-Ahab (Aḥav) (2 Kings 9:2,3,6-10 and 10:15-17). They are again heard from in the sixth century B.C.E. when the Babylonian siege of Jerusalem forces them to alter their living patterns and to accept urban life. With such powerful cult groups as the Nazirenes and Rekhabites, traditions were developed around narratives that preserved their beliefs about their origins and founders. This oral tradition was *the* truth because—to borrow a phrase from Kierkegaard—they *lived* it. Versions of that tradition would be cultivated and each version was a variation on a central theme. Some of the associations and cults often became powerful enough to affect the central governing body, as was the case with the Rekhabites in the vanguard of the political/religious upheaval in the Northern Kingdom of Israel, ca. 850 B.C.E.

Legatees of the Rekhabite tradition during the Second Commonwealth were the zealous Ḥasidim of the Maccabean Period (175 B.C.E.). After the destruction of the Kingdom of Judah in the sixth century B.C.E., a wave of new ideas from the East, notably Iran, was introduced into the Second Commonwealth, e.g., angelology and apocalyptic struggle between good and evil. With the Graeco-Macedonian conquest of the Persian Empire (330 B.C.E.), other elements were added to an increasingly volatile solution. For instance, the influential *Book of Daniel,* published circa 175 B.C.E. in the reign of Antiochus IV, with retrojections to early Persian rule, described "the last day" ushered in by a mashiaḥ, a legitimate ruler (9:25). But one "like a man," a celestial or cosmic redeemer and not just an earthly anointed being, will come riding on the clouds bringing an everlasting sovereignty (7:13). In addition, death will be conquered; there will be individual *bodily* resurrection, not just an ascension of the soul (12:12). These ecstatic visions were to fire the next three centuries of thought. Brotherhoods and confraternities amalgamated and regrouped even as their ideas were interchanged; some earlier groups were revived under new guild names and some secret orders still maintained their mysterious traditions. In the post-Maccabean Age, along with the monastic Essenes, there were unnamed antipriestly sects, hermitlike subgroups, and associations of ritual bathers who formalized the washing off of sin/disease; all such gave profound testimony to the decentralized nature of Judaic practice and belief. Some brotherhoods preached sensational forecasts and apocalyptism, with an eschatology (end-of-days ideology) that was ultimately to become powerful enough to be absorbed by related sects that had preserved an ancient idea of salvation—the yeshua-ists.[49] Most of the yeshua-ists believed that God would enter history directly as an actor, directing events and partaking of them in turn. With the legacy of GLGL and Makkedah, Joshua (Yehoshua) 10:14 expresses it aptly: "Surely, YHVH fought for Israel [on that day]."

This theological certitude of salvation (*yeshua*), carried by one or more groups through centuries of trial and testing, revived periodically to provide psychological release and consolation, to lodge ultimately in the group later to be known as messianists or christists. It was an enduring brotherhood with a burning zeal of conviction in triumph over death; sufficient to revolutionize and reduce the parent body from which it sprang.

Notes

Introduction

1. Geza Vermes, *Jesus the Jew* (New York: Macmillan Publishing Company, 1973), p. 155.
2. Mircea Eliade, *Cosmos and History* (New York: Harper and Row, Torchbook Edition, 1959), p. 39.

Savior Gods

3. James B. Pritchard, *The Ancient Near East* (Princeton, N.J.: Princeton University Press, 1958), p. 85.
4. Letter 58 to Paulinus 3, *A Select Library of Nicene and Post Nicene Fathers of the Christian Church,* 1890–1900, vol. 6, eds. Philip Schaff and Henry Wace, p. 120.

> Though he does not expressly say so, Jerome seems to have thought that the grove of Adonis [Tammuz] had been planted by the heathen after the birth of Christ for the purpose of defiling the sacred spot. In this he may have been mistaken. If Adonis was indeed . . . the spirit of the corn, a more suitable name for his dwelling place could hardly be found than Bethlehem, or "the House of Bread," and he may well have been worshipped there at his House of Bread long ages before the birth of Him who said, "I am the bread of life." (James G. Frazer, *The Golden Bough,* Abr. ed. [New York: Macmillan Company, 1951], p. 402)

5. Mircea Eliade, *Cosmos and History* (New York: Harper and Row, Torchbook Edition, 1959), p. 34.
6. William F. Albright, *From the Stone Age to Christianity* (Baltimore: The Johns Hopkins Press, 1946), p. 30.

The Tradition of Emperor Worship

7. F. C. Grant, *Ancient Roman Religion* (New York: Liberal Arts Press, 1957), p. 174.

A First-Century Holy Man Rival

8. F. C. Conybeare (trans.), *Philostratus: The Life of Apollonius of Tyana,* vol. 2 (Cambridge: Harvard University Press, 1948), p. 417.

9. Ibid., "The Treatise of Eusebius, The Son of Pamphilus Against the Life of Apollonius of Tyana Written by Philostratus, Occasioned by the Parallel Drawn by Hierocles Between Him and Christ," p. 491.

Josephus

10. Emil Schürer, *The Jewish People in the Time of Jesus* (New York: Schocken Books, 1961), p. 211. (Originally published in German; first English edition, 1886.)

11. Colm Luibhéid, *The Essential Eusebius* (New York: The New American Library, 1966), pp. 81–84.

12. *Epictetus: The Discourses as Reported by Arrian,* Book II, 18–22, trans. W. A. Oldfather (Cambridge: Harvard University Press, 1974), p. 273.

13. Luibhéid, *Eusebius* (*H.E.* III, 19–20), p. 107.

14. Luibhéid, *Eusebius* (*H.E.* III, 32:3), p. 116.

15. Josephus, *Wars of the Jews,* Book VII, 6:6 in *Josephus: Complete Works,* trans. William Whiston (Grand Rapids: Kregel Publications, 1981), p. 597.

> About the same time it was that Caesar . . . gave order that all Judea should be exposed to sale; for he did not found any city there, but reserved the country for himself. . . . He also laid a tribute upon the Jews wheresoever they were, and enjoined every one of them to bring two drachmae every year into the Capitol, as they used to pay the same to the temple at Jerusalem.

It seems that the tribute went to the private treasury of Vespasian himself, since the country was treated as his fiefdom!

16. *Suetonius, The Lives of the Caesars,* vol. 2, trans. J. C. Rolfe, Book VIII (Domitian XII) (Cambridge: Harvard University Press, 1950), p. 367.

17. H. St. John Thackeray, *Josephus: The Man and the Historian* (The Strook Lectures, 1929) (New York: Ktav Publishing House, 1967), pp. 143–53.

18. Solomon Zeitlin, *The Rise and Fall of the Judean State,* vol. 2 (Philadelphia: Jewish Publication Society, 1967), p. 374.

19. A. C. Bouquet, "The References to Josephus in the Bibliotheca of Photius," *The Journal of Theological Studies* 36 (1935): 289–91.

20. Cited in Robert McQueen Grant, *Eusebius as Church Historian* (Oxford: Oxford University Press, 1980), p. 103.

A similar statement is found in another of Origen's works, *Contra Celsum* I:47:

The same author [Josephus] although he did not believe in Jesus as Christ, sought for the cause of the fall of Jerusalem and the destruction of the temple. He ought to have said that the plot against Jesus was the reason why these catastrophes came upon the people, because they had killed the prophesied Christ; however, although unconscious of it, he is not far from the truth when he says that these disasters befell the Jews to avenge James the Just, who was a brother of "Jesus the so-called Christ," since they had killed him who was a very righteous man.

The translator notes that the theodicy concerning James may be a Christian interpolation, that it "does not occur in any extant MS of the *Antiquities* at the relevant place (*Antiq.* XX, 9, 1) or elsewhere." See note 2 in Henry Chadwick (trans.), *Origen: Contra Celsum,* I:47 (Cambridge, England: At the University Press, 1953), p. 43.

21. Luibhéid, *Eusebius* (*H.E.* II, 23:1–25), p. 88.
22. Grant, *Eusebius as Church Historian* (*H.E.* IV 22:8), p. 38.
23. Ibid. (*H.E.* I, 1.4), p. 28.
24. Schürer, p. 211.
25. Robert McQueen Grant, *A Historical Introduction to the New Testament* (New York: Harper and Row, 1963), p. 294.

Tacitus

26. "Theories that make Tacitus finish the Annals as early as 117 or 118 begin to look implausible. . . . Tacitus composed the great bulk [of the Annals] under Hadrian (117–138), not perhaps completing the eighteen books before the sixth year of that emperor. . . ." [i.e., 123 C.E.]. (Ronald Syme, *Tacitus,* Vol. 2 [Oxford: Oxford University Press, 1958], p. 473.
27. Syme, p. 469.
28. *Tacitus: The Annals,* Book XV, trans. John Jackson (XLIV 1–8) (Cambridge: Harvard University Press, 1956), p. 483.

The Annals represents the mature Tacitus, 117 C.E.ff; the *Histories* was written between 104–109 C.E. Between 113–116, Tacitus was serving as proconsul governing the province of Asia Minor. (Chronology is provided by Tacitus right within his works.)

Concerning events in the reign of the Emperor Tiberius, there is some difference between what Tacitus says in the *Annals* and what he says in the *Histories,* namely, "Under Tiberius, all was quiet [in Judaea]. But when the Jews were ordered by Caligula (37–41 C.E.) to set up his statue in the Temple, they preferred the alternative of war. The death of the Emperor put an end to the disturbance."

The selection from *Annals* suggests the checking of an incipient disturbance in the reign of Tiberius by a "death penalty." The selection from *Histories* speaks of "quiet."

See *Tacitus: The Annals and the Histories* (The Great Histories Series), trans. A. J. Church and W. J. Brodribb, ed. Hugh Lloyd Jones (New York: Washington Square Press, 1964), p. 452.

29. The inscription reads: "[Po]ntius Pilatus [Praef]ectus Iudae[ae]." Illustration no. 19 in Arnold Toynbee, *The Crucible of Christianity* (World Book Company, 1969).

30. *Lactantius: The Divine Institutes,* Book IV.7, trans. Sister Mary Francis McDonald (Washington, D.C.: The Catholic University Press, 1964), p. 258.

31. See note 27. Jackson, *Tacitus: The Annals,* p. 284, #2.

32. Edward Gibbon, *The Decline and Fall of the Roman Empire,* abr. ed. (New York: Gallery Books, 1979), p. 204.

33. William Whiston (trans.), *Josephus: Complete Works: Antiquities,* XX:5, and *Wars of the Jews* 13:5, p. 418.

34. "*Iudaeos impulsore Chresto assidue tumultuantis Roma expulit.*" The dating is according to Ronald Syme, *Tacitus* (Oxford: Oxford University Press, 1958), p. 781.

35. *Suetonius: The Lives of the Caesars,* vol. 2, trans. J. C. Rolfe, Book V (XXV) (Cambridge: Harvard University Press, 1959), p. 53.

36. Adolf Harnack, *The Mission and Expansion of Christianity in the First Three Centuries,* trans. and ed. James Moffatt (New York: Harper and Brothers, Harper Torchbooks, 1961), pp. 413–14.

37. Justin, "First Apology" (no. 4), in *Marcus Aurelius and His Times,* Walter J. Black (for the Classics Club) (Roslyn, New York), p. 261:

> Justin avails himself here of the similarity in sound of the Greek words *Christos* ("Christ") and *chrestos* ("good," "worthy," "excellent"). The play upon these words is kept up throughout this paragraph and cannot always be represented to the English reader.

38. Tertullian, *Apologeticus* II 3 (The Great Plea Addressed to Magistrates of the Empire), trans. T. R. Glover (Cambridge: Harvard University Press, Loeb Classical Library, 1958), p. 9.

> Tell me, then, if it is hatred of a name, how can you indict names? What charge can lie against words. . . . "Christian," so far as translation goes is derived from "anointing." Yes, and when it is mispronounced by you "Chrestian" . . . it is framed from "sweetness" or "kindness." (*Apologeticus* III:5, p. 21)

39. "The reason of this name ought to be explained on account of the error of those ignorant people who are accustomed to pronounce it *chrestus* by the change of a letter" (*Lactantius,* p. 258).

40. It is astounding to read that ". . . here is authentic evidence . . . of the early existence of a Christian community in Rome" (Donald R. Dudley, *The World of Tacitus* [Boston: Little, Brown and Company, 1968], p. 166) or that Tacitus registers the "origin of the name 'Christian' with 'documentary precision' " (Syme, p. 469).

41. Even Harnack, who believes that the term Christian was known by the reign of Trajan (98–117 C.E.), also says that it was not in common use earlier than the close of Hadrian's reign or Pius's reign, a difference of twenty-two years! "By the days of Trajan, the Christians of Asia Minor had probably been in possession of this title for a considerable period, but its general vogue cannot be dated earlier than the close of Hadrian's reign [138 C.E.] or that of [Antoninus] Pius [161 C.E.]" (Harnack, p. 412).

Sources of Jesus' Biography

42. *Lactantius: The Divine Institutes,* Book IV, trans. Sister Mary Francis McDonald (Washington, D.C.: The Catholic University Press, 1964), p. 289.

43. *Pseudepigrapha,* trans. W. J. Deane (1891), p. 312, cited in Thomas Whittaker, *The Origins of Christianity* (London: Watts & Co., n.d.), p. 30.

44. In the fourteenth-century B.C.E. *Amarna Letters,* the name of Joshua appears as *Ia-šu-ia* and in a Phoenician seal as *Yeshua.*

45. In 1 Samuel 31:10, the Philistines nailed the body of Saul the King to the wall at Beth Shan.

46. J. G. Frazer, *The Golden Bough,* abr. ed. (New York: Macmillan Company, 1951), p. 412.

47. Ibid., pp. 675–79.

Marginal Cults and Confraternities

48. In 1 Samuel 14, Prince Jonathan (Yonatan) unknowingly breaks the war taboo of not tasting food, and his father Saul, the king, wants to have him executed. In 2 Samuel 11, King David tries to conceal his sin in his affair with Bat-Sheva, wife of Uriah, one of his army captains. He has Uriah brought home from the battle front and bids him go home and "wash his feet" (a circumlocution for cohabiting with his wife). Uriah spends the night sleeping on the palace grounds because he is under the warrior code. Even after he is made drunk on David's order, Uriah does not go home to his wife.

49. For instance, early forms of gnosticism (pure spirit) were imported from abroad: the worship of the "spirit" of salvation. The Mandean Nazoreans or Sabaeans worshipped an Iranian god-man, Anosh Uthra, who was not a historical person but, again, some kind of spirit. Another sub-sect of Nazoreans (consecrated or separated ones) were also called Jesseans, the name deriving either from Jesse (Yishai), father of David, or from Yeshua ("Healer" or "Savior"). Before the fateful year 70 C.E., these mystery cults were simply Jewish sectarians, along with the more well-known Essenes, who were destroyed by the war with Rome, and the Ebionite cult, which, because of its Judaic ties, could not be absorbed into the later Christian faith community and hence disappeared.

3

Historicity in Tacit Belief

Cultural Prepossession

"Thy Kingdom Come" is a prayer; it is not the recording of a historical event. It amounts to uttering "may it be thy will," which most will recognize as distinct from what the situation in fact *is*. Critical readers of gospel writings become aware of the sparseness of detail, the variation, and even conflict in accounts (e.g., the genealogy of Jesus according to Matthew and Luke). Yet, despite their skeletal structures, historical truth—however grudging—has been granted to them, often simply on the basis of an order of presentation. Willy-nilly, the reader—in thought process—constructs chronology involuntarily and reflexively: the precedent and the subsequent, *this* before *that, that* as a consequence of *this*. Even when subjected to critical analysis, gospel writings are, nevertheless, the starting point for what may be termed "historicity in tacit belief or silent agreement."

The summary statements presented here are intended to indicate the lingering hold of a "yes, but . . ." argument, even when the conclusions are recognized as possessing coherent validity: There is *no* source material on the person named Jesus *from the period* of his sojourn on earth. What we presume to know of his existence does not come from non-Christian sources such as Josephus or Tacitus, but from what is presented in gospel writings, which are distant from him both in time and place.[1] Gospel writings are not contemporaneous reports nor is their style a narrative account. Their composition reflects unknown multiple authorship, attached to the names of disciples or associates of disciples, and all written outside the land in which the events purportedly took place: Mark and Luke in Rome; Matthew in Antioch, Syria; and John in Ephesus, Western Asia. While the language in which a rural Galilaean national would have expressed himself was Aramaic, the literature composed about Jesus by subsequent and educated endorsers was in Greek. The remark contained in the Papias fragment regarding the work of Matthew is recalled here: "So Matthew composed the sayings in the Aramic language, and everyone translated them as well as he could. . . ."[2] The writings of the influential missionary Paul—the letters to Romans, 1 and 2 Corinthians, and Galatians considered authentically Pauline, antedating gospel writings at the turn of the first century and later—were also composed in Greek; this is understandable since the letters were addressed to communities outside Judaea. Even when critical scholarship agrees that the record of a Jesus is largely the imaginative life story of his followers and their theologizing activities, a "last ditch" defense arises from within the very act of thought itself: there *has* to be a kernel of truth, albeit symbolic, within the constructions. One cannot concur with Rudolf Bultmann's view that the message of Christianity lies *outside* history—a suprahistory. Too many claims on the *record* have been made and too much anchoring in time and place has occurred: "In those days a decree was issued by the Emperor Augustus for a census . . . it took place *when* Quirinus was governor of Syria . . . Joseph went up to *Judaea* from the town of *Nazareth* in Galilee, to register in the *city of David* called Bethlehem . . ." (emphases added) (Luke 2:1–5). Such citations and re-citations have riveted time and place in the minds of scholarly and mass thought alike, to the point where a "persistent *petitio principii*" (to use J. M. Robertson's felicitous phrase)[3] grips otherwise highly disciplined thinkers. Since matters geographical are basic to the "persistent *petitio*," it is well to consider them.

Geographical Locations

The "city of David" is, of course, Jerusalem and not Bethlehem, Bethlehem being referred to as a granary, but this is relatively minor alongside the obscurity of a location called Nazareth, especially when linked descriptively to Jesus *of* Nazareth. The argument for the existence of a village by the name of Nazareth is a strange one. One may note the ongoing dispute over the location of Mount Sinai: Was Kadesh Barnea, in the Wilderness of Zin, the main camping site of the ancient Israelites in the nothern Negev Desert? Was the mountain called Horeb the same as Jebel Sirbal or Jebel Musa in Southeast Sinai, or was it in the land, Seir, beyond the Jordan River and Dead Sea? Or, was it, perhaps, in the northern part of Saudi Arabia? A similar dispute rages over the location of a frequently named site called Tarshish, which is transferred from one location to another. Is it in Asia Minor, Etruria, Sardinia, or Spain, or in all of these? Yet, the existence of Nazareth is simply taken for granted. Even though the place name is unmentioned in the Old Testament, or in Josephus, or in the Talmud, we seem to possess a cultural memory that Nazareth was the scene of Jesus' boyhood, the silence of contemporary sources of the first few centuries C.E. actually being taken as *evidence* of its existence as a locality.

Well might we ask: *When* was the date of the first map showing Nazareth? In *The Christian Topography,* written in 535 to 547 C.E. by an Alexandrian monk named Cosmas, we find the following declaration: "It contains in all probability the oldest Christian maps that have survived." The "maps" are more charts of faith than of terrain, and reflect a faith view of the world.[4] Until the eighteenth century, maps, reprints, and cartographers' drawings had to rely upon an oral tradition and upon Queen Mother Helena's fourth century C.E. visit to Galilee and upon her understanding of gospel writings. The mother of Constantine the Great determined the location of the principal events in the earthly life of Jesus and commemorated them with funds from the imperial treasury. Nazareth (Natzrat in Hebrew) appears only in the sixth century C.E. as a definite name and place, with the conversion of a synagogue building into a church, according to the *Encyclopaedia of Archaeological Excavations in the Holy Land.*[5] The name also appears in a seventh-century poem by Eliezer Kallir. However, according to the renowned Bible scholar George Adam Smith, author of the *Historical Geography of the Holy Land,* Nazareth was a secluded and obscure village ". . . proved by the silence of the gospels concerning His [Jesus'] childhood and youth."[6] Now, an argument of silence is most often dismissed out-of-hand, especially if it questions the actual human existence of Jesus *of* Nazareth, but in this instance, silence is regarded as proof. George Adam Smith said elsewhere: "The value of a vision of the Holy Land is that it fills in the silences."[7]

Outside gospel writings, Nazareth is mentioned by Eusebius in the fourth-century C.E. *Onomasticon* 138.24 as a small *Jewish* village.[8] In a non-Christian work of the same century, Nazareth appears "in an inscription in the synagogue of Caesaresa which lists twenty-four priestly families that settled in Galilee."[9] However, at the time of Eusebius's mention, there were only three *Christian* villages in the whole country of Palestine, while Christian communities existed within urban settlements such as Lydda, Jaffa, Sebaste, Scythopolis, Ascalon, Gaza, and Jericho.[10]

A related problem for the geographer is the precise location of the reputed ministerial site of Capernaum (Kefar Naḥum). The corrupted pronunciation "Capurnium" is the equivalent of the sailor's "Billy Ruffian" for Bellerophon. In the *Life of Flavius Josephus,* #72, Josephus relates how—because of an injury in the War of 66 C.E.—he was removed for a short interval to a village named *Cepharnome* or *Capernaum*, before being taken further behind the battle front for treatment. In his *Wars of the Jews*, III, 10:8, however, Josephus refers to a *fountain* called *Caphar.um* near Lake Gennesareth (Sea of Galilee). The "fountain" is ment.oned in Zechariah 13:1,2 as a place where sin and impurity will be removed. It is also noteworthy that verses 2–6 warn against prophets and their robes of coarse hair ("in order to deceive"): "I shall also expel the prophets and the spirit of uncleanness from the land." In *The Gospel According to Mark* (1:21ff), the symbolism of Zechariah's fountain appears as a town with a synagogue, from which an unclean spirit is cast out. It is generally agreed that the synagogue was essentially a diaspora institution (in Babylon and Egypt), not diffused within Judaea and Galilee, prior to the destruction of the Temple at Jerusalem in 70 C.E. With the exception of the palace and fortress sites unearthed at Metsada, Herodium, and Gamla, and the claims put forward that buildings within them (such as the dining room at Herodium) served as places of worship by the Zealots in the War of 66–73 C.E., there are no distinct architectural edifices known as *synagogues* dating from the *first* century. Typically, it was a large room in a private house that served as a gathering place, Philo even referring to such as "meeting houses"; yet, it is not entirely clear whether it was the *act* of meeting or the *place* of meeting that was indicated.

Sometimes prepossessions are buried under a stratum of archaeological nomenclature, suggesting scientific support of a claim. That prepossession can distort vision is evident in two works devoted to the interpretation of archaeological findings. The first selection highlights a verse in Luke 7:5: ". . . he is a friend of our nation and it is he who built our synagogue." Then, archaeological evidence regarding this synagogue is set forth:

> Among the ruins of ancient Capernaum the most imposing is that of a synagogue built about 200 A.D. . . . Since the custom was to build a new synagogue precisely on the site of a previous one (Maimonides stated that such was the tradition), one may assume that this synagogue was located at the same place as the one at the time of Jesus. A limited excavation in 1953–54 made under the synagogue's southeastern corner uncovered some black basalt blocks which are probably part of the foundation of the synagogue which Jesus attended and which was possibly the one given by the friendly Roman centurion [mentioned in Luke 7:5] to the Jews.[11]

The data clearly indicate that a synagogue was erected at the beginning of the third century C.E. The author's preconceptions lead him to claim something over and beyond this. What is asserted without warrant may be denied without warrant!

A related selection, in a different work, tells of a house on the shore of the Sea of Galilee believed to be the site of Peter's home and of early Christian worship. (If verified as such, it would be the oldest Christian sanctuary.) On the ruins of the house was built a chapel, occupied by Franciscans since the 1940s; indeed, the church built over the ruins had an architectural style reserved for sacred sites, and was considered as part of the corroborative evidence. Included as support for the claim is the tradition of fourth-century pilgrims who identified the site as Peter's house; etched crosses and graffiti in Greek, Hebrew, and Aramaic; Herodian coins attesting to the century of construction; and the finding of fishhooks beneath the pavement of the house. Regarding the latter, the author declares naively that "it is conceivable that a fisherman lived here." In the eager attempt to offer *authentic* evidence, what gets uncovered is—prepossession. Even the author avers: "This possibility [the house of Peter] is so remarkable that it elicits from an audience the charge of slipping from the rigors of scholarship into sensationalism. Yet it is not the claim, but the discovery, which may well be sensational."[12]

Given the human predilection to credulousness and to leaping beyond the data, it is not to be wondered at that archaeological evidence has revealed an error of several miles in Queen Mother Helena's siting of the holy place at Capernaum (in the fourth century C.E.). One notes also that it was under her leadership that the cave of nativity at Bethlehem was identified in 326 C.E. and the Church of Nativity then erected.[13] She piously— if not authoritatively—located many other sites mentioned in gospel writings (e.g., the Tomb of Jesus) and these have been absorbed in cultural memory as inspirationally—if not topographically—actual and accurate locations.[14]

Departing Capernaum, and returning now to a site called Nazareth, and the absence of solid first-century geographical evidence for it, there are several hypotheses worth considering regarding the origin of its name. Some hold that it may derive from *nesoret* or "sawdust," as Gennesareth refers to the valley of *sawyers,* the connection to the trade of carpentry being obvious. (The alteration of the second consonant, *tz* to a *z* sound is a common one.) Then, *nazareth*—properly pronounced with the hard *z* (*tz*)—may be a derivative of *netzer* (a "branch" or "shoot"), which would be in keeping with a genealogical claim to descent from the House of David and the prophetic references to a "shoot," particularly in Isaiah (Yesha-*yahu*) 11:1. Some see the origin of the term *nazarenes* or more properly, nazirenes, as a corruption of *netzerenes,* literally *branch-ists,* or, later, messianists or christ-ists. However, there are two distinct terms (and consonants) in Hebrew: *netzer,* spelled and pronounced with the hard *z* sound, meaning "plant" or "branch"; and *nazir,* spelled and pronounced with a soft *z* sound, meaning "separated" or "consecrated one." More likely is the hypothesis that the origin stems from the old brotherhood, *nazir* (consecrated), as in Nazirenes or Nazoreans, a long-standing association in Israel (see p. 67). Thus, *nazareth* would represent an assimilation of sounds (*z* and *tz*), altering the original pronunciation of the name. Matthew 2:23 reveals this sound assimilation very clearly: ". . . . he [Joseph] settled in a town called Naz[*tz*]areth. This was to fulfill the words spoken through the prophets: 'He shall be called a Naz[*z*]arene.'" It is well to point out that some of the early Judaeo-Christians were called by the composite name Nazarene or Natzorean (e.g., the Ebionites or poor ones). Even the title said to be inscribed over a cross of crucifixion bore the legend "iesus nazarenus," and again, the peculiar problem becomes either to assimilate *nazirene* (separated one) with *nazareth* (branch) or to distinguish the two terms, as the Hebrew spelling, pronunciation, and meaning certainly does. Whatever the origin of the designation, as the name Jesus itself may be an objectification of the concept of salvation or *yeshua,* so *nazareth* can be reconstructed into a geographical site by the same processs of objectification of a *consecrated branch of Jesse* (*Nezir, netzer Yishai.*)

The common usage, Jesus *OF* Nazareth, may be a reflection of all that has just been set forth, the expression gaining currency because of a later geographical location. Was there a village by the name of Nazareth in the early first century? Initially, we have an adjective whose precise origin is obscure, representing a compound of more than one concept: a *nazir* or consecrated one, and a *netzer,* a branch or shoot. *Nazareth* may simply be a combination of *nazirene* and *netzerene* (or *natzorean*). Matthew 2:23 reveals the totally indiscriminate use of *nazarene* and *nazareth*. Indeed, in the Gideon Bible, in Mark 1:23, 24, a man with an unclean spirit cries out against Jesus: "What business is it of yours to bother us, Jesus You Nazarene?" The same verse in the Revised English Bible reads: "What do you want with us, Jesus of Nazareth?"

If the expression Jesus the Nazirite or Jesus the Natzorean is regarded as a strange one, it has the justification of being within the tradition of Jesus the Nazarene with its familiar ring. Furthermore, Jesus the Nazirite (or Jesus the Natzorean) expresses a similar adjectival intent as Jesus the Nazarene, and it may be recognized as a claim, either to membership in an ancient brotherhood or to an honorific genealogy or to some fusion of the two claims. The readily familiar Jesus *OF* Nazareth—which seems to trip off the tongue so easily—obscures important critical considerations, and tendentiously offers us a geographical site in which to deposit what is essentially a theological argument. What has been said here requires a reversal in thought: The theological ideas and claims formed the basis for naming a locality in Galilee.

We go on now to Gilgal (see p. 64), 1¼ miles from Jericho (Yeriḥo), for yet another geographical excursus which bears heavily on the historicity of an actual person. In *The Lost Tribes: A Myth,* author Allen Godbey refers to Gilgal as an altar or cromlech of rough stones: "Any Gilgal was a prominent sanctuary from Joshua's time on . . . [t]he earthen altars in any Gilgal [circular altar] are as numerous as the ridges in a plowed field."[15] The circle of stones that Joshua (Yehoshua) raised as a memorial not far from Jericho (Yeriḥo) was, no doubt, the origin of the place name itself. To point out that the Hebrew consonants alone, read GLGL, is to indicate that they can be vocalized in a variety of ways: G*i*lg*a*l (circle or rolling), G*a*lg*a*l or G*a*lg*o*l (wheel, g*u*lg*o*l[eth] (skull). (The consonant *t* or *th* is a grammatical form only, indicating whether a noun is masculine or feminine; the consonant *t* does not affect the general meaning of the term.) In Judges 9:53, concerning the would-be-king Abi-melekh, a woman throws a millstone from a tower at him and breaks his skull g*u*lgolto), the possessive "his" indicated by the suffix vowel o̅. Second Kings 9:35 describes the death of Queen Jezebel (Izevel): all that remains of the body is the skull (g*u*lgol[eth]). The relationship between the three words with four identical primary consonants (GLGL [*T*]) and the fifth indicating grammatical gender only, is of significance in locating Golgotha (Place of a "Skull") given in *The Gospel According to Matthew* 27:33 (and Mark 15:22), as the site of crucifixion of Jesus. In *The Gospel According to Luke* 23:33, the site is referred to simply as "skull," with the Latin *Calvaria* (Calvary) also translating as "skull." Since, outside of gospel writings, it was unknown, where was this place? It took three centuries for piety to locate it and to mark it. Under order of Emperor Constantine, a basilica (the Church of the Holy Sepulcher) was erected in Jerusalem and dedicated in 335 C.E. on the thirtieth anniversary of Constantine's reign. The events concerning construction and dedication of the church(es) are described in detail by Eusebius who—be it noted—speaks of the tomb of Jesus but says nothing of crucifixion in his *Life of Constantine,* iv: 40–47.[16] Constantine's architects gave attention to two key points: the rock of Calvary (Golgotha) and the Tomb of Jesus (which was to become the Church of Anastasis or Resurrection). The words in the itinerary of the *Bordeaux Pilgrim* who visited Jerusalem in 333 C.E. read: "On the left hand is the little hill of Golgotha where the Lord was crucified. About a stone's throw from there is a vault wherein his body was laid and rose again on the third day."[17] About this itinerary, the author notes: "This was drawn up in 333 A.D. and was the work of a Christian being intended for the use of pilgrims on their way from Western Europe to Jerusalem. Its starting point is Burdigala (Bordeaux) . . . it is the earliest description we have of the Holy Places."[18]

As is known, the Church of the Holy Sepulcher was destroyed by the Persians in 614 C.E. and later rebuilt ca. 1050 C.E. A hill north of the present Jerusalem city wall, known as Gordon's Calvary, has *also* been identified as the site of crucifixion on the basis of its 1842 C.E. appearance as a skull (to Pastor Otto Thenius of Dresden, Germany), which theory was adopted by General Gordon of Khartoum fame. Nearby, the Garden Tomb (under Anglican auspices) has also been fixed as the burial place of Jesus. Both of these sites lie outside the walls of the city of Jerusalem of the first century.

Such exertions in locating a holy site may be quixotic, since *Golgotha* is an invented explanation derived from a linguistic and not a topographical source, i.e., GLGLT (*Gulgolet* in Hebrew and its cognate in Aramaic GLGLTA [*Gulgolta*]), the vowel sound *a* being an ordinary Aramaic ending.[19] Since the middle *l* consonant of Gulgo*l*ta probably became swallowed in pronunciation, it was simply elided in spelling as well, giving us *Gulgota* or *Gulgotha*. With further vowel alteration, whether in dialect or assimilation of sound, *gulgotha* orthographically became *golgotha*. The connection to GLGL is highly suggestive: the original *Gilgal* or *Galgol* was named for the circular shape of an altar of stones which became a military encampment and subsequently, the site of a cultic shrine (to be outranked by Shiloh) where a confraternity preserved the memory of kings sacrificed or executed by hanging from trees. In addition to the citations of chapter 10 of the Book of Joshua, recording such sacrificial executions, it is well to note that a later ritual execution of the king of Amalek by the prophet Samuel took place at Gilgal: "Then Samuel hewed Agag in pieces before YHVH . . ."; the "hewing" and the phrase "before YHVH" suggesting sacrifice (1 Samuel 15:32–33).

By the eighth century B.C.E., the associated cultic practices at the shrine of GLGL led to severe condemnation by the prophets (see p. 64). However, preservation of a cultural memory of GLGL through its collegia was conjoined with a fervent desire for salvation personified. *Golgotha* was not an identifiable hillock, whether inside or outside the walls of Jerusalem, the Queen Mother Helena, the Bordeaux Pilgrim, or General Gordon notwithstanding. As a reminder of the shrine at GLGL, it became part of the process of objectification; a cultural memory preserved the theme of sacrificial execution and "the place" was transposed from *there* to *here,* from *then* to *now.*

The Error of Homologization

It is easily understood that the replacement of a mark in the flesh, such as a tattoo, is difficult. How much more difficult is a tattoo in one's thoughts?

Even the common American tendency to convert the metric system (kilometers into miles) is an example of the difficulty. Certainly, the convictions concerning Golgotha and Nazareth are well-nigh impregnable because the addition of granite and the art of the mason has created a spatial and temporal reality, sealing within it problems of nomenclature and its origins.

What energy source feeds the "yes, but . . . " argument in producing its viselike effect? As noted earlier, J. M. Robertson had characterized it as the "persistent *petitio principii,*" the inability to unloosen ingrained presuppositions. This is an apt characterization, but it does not fully describe how the paralyzing effect ensues. What is the manner in which the "yes, but . . ." argument gets presented?

The prodigious intellect of John Stuart Mill declared:

> Who among his disciples or among their proselytes was capable of inventing the sayings ascribed to Jesus, or of imagining the life and character revealed in the Gospels? Certainly not the fishermen of Galilee; as certainly not St. Paul . . .; still less the early Christian writers in whom nothing is more evident than that the good which was in them was all derived, as they always professed that it was derived from the higher source. . . . The East was full of men who could have stolen any quantity of this poor stuff [the mystical parts of *The Gospel According to John*] as the multitudinous sects of Gnostics afterward did. But about the life and sayings of Jesus there is a stamp of personal originality combined with profundity of insight. . . .[20]

The trouble (for most people, along with Mill) begins at the point of *entry* of focus: viewing the final written edifice of Christianity as if it were *one* composition, perhaps the product of a divine theography, and not the result of a school, i.e., multiple authorship over a period of two to three centuries of retouchings and refinements. The common tendency is to homologize all the literature under one rubric and to attribute it to a *single* source and then to ask naively: Could Galilaean fishermen produce gospel writings? Could Paul? Indeed, Paul could not, since his life was ended eighty to ninety years before gospel writings were to be connected to each other in any systematic way. Moreover, Paul—in his Letters, the question of pseudepigraphy apart—was conspicuously silent about a living Jesus or any *living* incident appertaining to his person, *including* his death, or the incidents related thereunto. For Paul, it is only with his *death* that he becomes "alive" as the risen Redeemer. In fact, these older[21] canonical Christian writings are uninterested in an earthly biography at all!

If the point of entry of focus of a Mill were to the Papias fragments,

Interpretations of the Sayings of the Lord, the product of the first generation of apostles' disciples, one might be more taken with the primitiveness of the *Sayings.* Indeed, the learned and opulent Bishop Eusebius, two centuries later, considered Papias stupid and looked upon his earnest efforts with haughty contempt. It is not certain whether Eusebius's contemptuousness was the result of a respected, imperial position in a now triumphalist, resplendent, and glittering Church (325 C.E.), or whether he was embarrassed that Papias had let a secret out: the very humble origins and repetitions of learned and folk wisdom contained in his *Sayings.* Surely, a statement such as: "So Matthew composed the Sayings in the Aramaic language, and everyone translated them as well as he could"[22] is not a particularly impressive endorsement of *The Gospel According to Matthew*—at least not to a bishop with an imperial commission!

To Mill's rhetorical assertion, *who* could produce such profundity and originality? A simple answer suffices. In the second century C.E. of the Judaeo-Hellenistic culture in the Roman Empire, there was enough collective intellectual power to synthesize into an art-form loose religious doctrine and the free-floating ideas of centuries: magic and marvel, messianism, redemptive sacrifice, conquest of earth, bodily resurrection, universalism, emigration from wretchedness, and residence in a heavenly city, as a haven for believers. To compose a mosaic of fragments and phrases from Scriptural sources is essentially a literary device employed widely in early medieval Jewish, Christian, and Islamic poetry and prose. Furthermore, the massive enterprise of micro-examination of the Old Testament in order to find disparate sayings that could be connected to a theory of prediction (such as the Suffering Servant in Isaiah 53, the colt of a donkey in Zechariah 9:19 for regal entry into the city, "[t]hey share out my clothes among them and cast lots for my garments" in Psalms 22:18, and the vinegar drink in Psalm 69:21) culminating in a supplemental counter-Scriptures, called the *New Testament, required centuries of effort (200 B.C.E.–200 C.E.),* and thousands upon thousands of readers and scribes. As is known from the finding of the Dead Sea Scrolls in 1947, a whole guild of copyists and scribes spent their entire lives in recording and reproducing earlier works (as yet, there was no printing press, let alone copying machines). Thus, if only *one* individual could author the material contained in New Testament writings, it would not have had the force and impact that it did have in its day.

A well-recognized scholar of intertestamental literature made the same kind of error that Mill did. Samuel Sandmel writes in *We Jews and Jesus:*

> . . . a Jewish person, for all that he would agree with [David Friedrich] Strauss that the Gospels are replete with legends and contradic-

tions, would nevertheless hold to the opinion that Gospels and Talmud are similar weavings of similar threads and such a person would say to a [Bruno] Bauer [who finds no history in them] that no imagination could out of thin air create so authentically, the religious scene and the flavor of Palestinian Judaism. Such a Jew would be prone to say that however wrong this or that detail of the Gospels may be, the general overall impression of a conformity to the general facts is indisputable. To this opinion I myself subscribe.[23]

If one were to ask what are the "general facts" that are being alluded to, the response would likely be: the life and death of Jesus the Nazirite. As for "this or that detail," it suffices to mention but a few, which at the very least reveal that gospel writings were very far from eyewitness reports and that their composition took place much later than is generally believed.

A title that had fallen into disuse at least three hundred years before the first century was "prophet," since there no longer was a prophetic function—i.e., revelation of God's will—to mankind in the period of the Second Jewish Commonwealth (516 B.C.E.–70 C.E.). The Book of Prophets (and prophecy) was officially closed in the fifth century B.C.E. with the writings of Haggai, Zechariah, and Malachi (see Zechariah 13:2–6 on the expulsion of prophets!) Thereafter, priests came to the fore in religious leadership. When the *Book of Daniel* came to be written some time in the second century B.C.E., it posed a special problem, and Jewish and Christian treatment thereof is very revealing. It had a political purpose: to encourage resistance to the rule of the Seleucid Dynasty (Antiochus IV) by outlining a glorious future, and it presented suffering as a fact of Jewish history, both individual and national, providing a backdrop to the picture of a suffering servant. Moreover, Daniel was the only one of the thirty-nine books in the Jewish Canon (*Tanak*) with an *explicit* reference to bodily resurrection; it was not placed in the *Prophets* section of the canon, but rather in the third division known as *Writings*. In marked contrast, since the ideas expressed in Daniel were central to later Christian theology as it came to develop, the book was given a place of prominence in the Christian canon, being grouped with the three major prophets: Isaiah, Jeremiah, and Ezekiel. Daniel was viewed as prediction, written in the sixth century B.C.E., because events relating to Nebuchadnezzar are presented therein. The interpretation of apocalypse as prophecy was decisive in its long-range implications. Clearly, the status of prophecy and prophet reveals a major point of difference between the two faiths.

By the first century C.E., then, the designation "prophet" had acquired distinctly pejorative overtones, as indicated in Josephus (Book XX) where prophets are regarded as deceivers and pretenders who played on popular credulity, as for example, Theudas (see p. 60). The prophet was looked upon quite differently in gospel writings; in Matthew 21:11, 45, it appears as a respected title. Through the centuries, it became very popular to speak of the prophet from Nazareth or Galilee. One finds it frequently in the nineteenth century, for example, in Mill's *Three Essays on Religion* (p. 254); in the twentieth century, it is the proud title of Morton Enslin's book *The Prophet from Nazareth.* It may be noted that tendentious argument can be located in such blithe usages: prophecy itself and the tradition of prophets is located in the new or successor Israel. In fact, the sculpting of the image of Jesus is as successor to the wonder-working prophets, Elijah (Eli-*yahu*) and Elisha; the tales of marvels and miracle cures woven about these legendary figures were part of the fabric of northern Israel for centuries.

It has been mentioned that religious leadership in the days of the Second Jewish Commonwealth resided with the priestly class. Alongside this hereditary aristocracy, in the first century B.C.E. a new group of leaders began to arise in religious and political opposition: teachers of the Law. These teachers were referred to by first names alone: Hillel, Shammai, Shemaya, Avtalyon, and others. With the destruction of the Temple in 70 C.E. came the demise of the priestly hierarchy. Still, matters of Jewish law had to be decided, and so investiture with the title of *Rav* came into being. The first titled *Rabban* was Yohanan ben Zakkai, who witnessed the destruction of Jerusalem and founded an academy of higher learning to train future teachers. Subsequently, the title involved authorization to decide matters of religious law, e.g., Gamaliel II.

The application of the title *Rabbi* (more properly *Rabee*) to Jesus in gospel writings (Mark 10:51, 14:45) reveals a clear "throwback" in time; it simply was not in currency before the year 70. (It may be noted that the anglicized pronunciation of the last vowel sound, *i,* cannot convey the devotion contained in the Hebrew pronunciation, *Rabee: My* teacher.[24])

Finally, is it a matter of small detail to note the sequential ordering in the New Testament? One may wonder at the phenomenon of historicizing. How and why does it occur? That retrojection and anachronism are democratically diffused may be linked to the way in which the mind is directed, i.e., the way history is read *into* a listing of events, sometimes on the basis of an author's sequence: since chapter 5 comes after chapter 1, it is evident that events described in chapter 5 are later than those in chapter 1! Thus, one can suppose that gospel writings precede Paul's Letters when, in fact, it is the reverse. (See note 21, p. 98.) Similarly, one may suppose that *The Gospel According to Matthew* was composed before that of Mark. Again, the reverse is the case. The placement may have been done because Matthew was said to have reflected the Aramaic language (the native tongue of Jesus' disciples), thereby making it more authentic.

Let us move now to the "thin air" in which pure imagination would have to operate, according to Sandmel. This is but a bubble structure, as the air in the first and second centuries C.E. was certainly not thin. Free play of the *collective* imagination was typical of the atmospheric condition and general milieu; the air was *thick* with supernatural tales relating to the idea of salvation (*yeshua*) and there were many marginal Judaisms, e.g., the sizable group of apocalyptists who thought that historical time had ended (the eschaton) or was about to end.[25] Sandmel asks further: ". . . do passages in the New Testament make more sense by assuming there was a Jesus than by denying it?" (p. 80). The implication is, of course, that such an invention—even of the collective imagination— could not be spun out. Surely, the human mind is capable of fancies of all sorts, viz., the character Robinson Crusoe, to whom some assign existentiality, or Mark 6:17-29. (See pp. 102-103.) Better yet, the Roman Jupiter had his temples, faithful priests, and votaries. Why is *this* deity deniable as metaphysical reality? At best, the argument of "making more sense" is an indirect one. It is akin to saying that the play *William Tell* "makes more sense" by assuming that he lived rather than that he did not. Otherwise, how could we account for the Swiss Confederation—a very strange asseveration? William Tell, of course, did not exist (despite Schiller and Rossini) and the Swiss Confederation was created without him.

For the mass of humankind, the existence of an actual person is a given reality the doubting of which would question the very existence of a self. In the implanting and embedding of this thought structure, gospel writings have, indeed, been successful; they do not inform, they convert to the doctrine that there is a reality *outside* history. The celebrated archaeologist W. F. Albright presents the idea with such force and clarity that it is worth citing at length:

> Because of their highly intimate and personal character some of them [the Gospels] are set forever beyond the reach of the critical historian, within whose epistemological range they cannot be drawn. In other words, the historian cannot control the details of Jesus's birth and resurrection and thus has no right to pass judgment on their historicity. On the other hand, the historian is qualified to estimate the historical significance of the pattern and its vital importance to the nascent Christian movement as embodied in the person of its Master. . . . It follows that the historian must recognize the presence of an important factual element in the Christian adaptation of the messianic tradition. Since, accordingly,

there can be no complete factual judgment and since the historian cannot settle questions which are outside his jurisdiction, the decision must be left to the Church and to the individual believer who are historically warranted in accepting the whole of the messianic framework of the Gospels or in regarding it as partly true literally and as partly true spiritually—which is far more important in the region of the spirit with which the Christian faith must primarily deal. The historian *quâ* historian must stop at the threshold, unable to enter the shrine of the Christian *mystêria* without removing his shoes, conscious that there are realms where history and nature are inadequate, and where God reigns over them in eternal majesty.[26]

This charter-like declaration relieves followers of a revealed faith from having to set forth historical evidence and such a *petitio* comes from a scientific researcher whose discipline demands hard, physical evidence in stone! As has been stated previously, not *one* date in gospel writings can be corroborated by a nonpartisan record—either of date of birth or date of death; one would surely settle for the bare outline of an obituary notice in the absence of a biography. Albright does indeed present us with a mystery: the indecipherable nature of divine actions. Evidence for the humanity of a person—on a human standard—cannot be produced, because if the person is *really* a divine being, then he is exempt from such standards. Thus, an action such as bodily resurrection—as a nonhistorical or suprahistorical happening—lies outside historical method. Well and good! Are we, then, readily equipped to distinguish the historical claim from the suprahistorical one? At which of the following are we to "take off our shoes"?

(1) God has incarnated himself into human flesh by experiencing the *mystêria* of birth and death.

(2) Joseph went up *to* Judaea *from* the town of Nazareth *in* Galilee *to* register *in* the city of David called Bethlehem . . . *when* Quirinus was governor of Syria (*The Gospel According to Luke* 2:1-5).

Ostensibly, the second records a given time and place—a historical claim. Yet, it too has been exempted from the usual requirements of empirical demonstration. While it is precisely the *humanity* of a Jesus that requires demonstration, the first centuries of the common era are fully loaded with theological disputes over divinity and its exact nature. It is as if statement number 2 above were to be abandoned in favor of number 1. (One can only guess at the reason.) Wellhausen's famous remark that without his death Jesus would not have become a personality at all reveals the nature of the problem: the historical claim to an "ordinary" existence is applicable; since it is exempt from demonstration, it is simply to be presupposed. The selection from Albright demonstrates admirably the theme of cultural prepossession and its viselike grip on thought: gospel writings are the starting point for historicity in tacit belief or silent agreement; they are the energy source that fuels the "yes, but . . ." argument. A historian has no right to pass judgment on their historicity because they are products of a theography. This brings us to a consideration of *kerygma,* the Proclamation of Faith of the theologians.[27]

Kerygma Rather Than Historicity

The first "modern" to utilize the idea found in the prophet Habakkuk 2:4[28] was Paul, and to understand him is to understand *kerygma* (literally, "proclamation"). (There will be consideration of his genius in chapter 4.) Kerygma may be characterized as the revelation of saving acts (*yeshua*) over which there is no human *intellectual* control; thus, it is distinct from "events" in history, in turn preclusive of the possible application of scientific methods to such "happenings." Any attempt to investigate beyond the proclamation is simply a refusal of belief, an attempt to gain control over God as it were.[29] In essence, kerygma theology is a dehistoricizing view, a chief exponent of which is Rudolf Bultmann.

In *Jesus Christ and Mythology,* Bultmann declares: "Christian preaching is *kerygma,* that is, a proclamation addressed not to the theoretical reason but to the hearer as a self."[30] It is the *Christ-event* as happening *here* and *now* for me. That event takes on objective reality only when and where the Proclamation confronts me and effects a change in my understanding.[31] This appears to be in the Kierkegaardian and Heideggerian tradition, which views the Bible not as historical document, but as ongoing revelation addressed to us now, something akin to a spiritual infusion. The popular evangelical preacher Billy Graham presents much the same message.

Bultmann continues:

This living word of God is not invented by the human spirit and by human sagacity; *it rises up in history.* [Emphasis added] Its origin is an historical event, by which the speaking of this word, the preaching, is rendered authoritative and legitimate. This event is Jesus Christ.

We may say that this assertion is paradoxical. For what God has done in Jesus Christ is not a historical fact which is capable of historical proof. The objectifying historian as such cannot see that a historical person (Jesus of Nazareth) is the eternal Logos, the Word. It is precisely the mythological description of Jesus Christ in the New Testament which makes it clear that the figure and the work of Jesus Christ must be understood in a manner which is beyond the categories by which the objective historian understands world history, if the figure and the work of Jesus Christ are to be understood as the divine work of redemption. . . .

According to the New Testament the decisive significance of Jesus Christ is that he—in his person,—his coming, his passion, and his glorification—is the eschatological event.[32]

To Bultmann's credit, he grants the paradoxical point: The *origin* of the Christ-event is historical, but the event itself eludes historical demonstration. "That God has acted in Jesus Christ is, however, not a fact of history open to historical verification."[33] Elsewhere he writes: "How uncertain is all knowledge of 'the historical Jesus'! Is he really within the scope of our knowledge? Here research ends with a large question mark —and here it *ought* to end."[34] Further on, he tells us why Jesus is not within the scope of our knowledge:

The facts which historical criticism can verify cannot exhaust, indeed they cannot adequately indicate, all that Jesus means to me. How he actually originated matters little, indeed we can associate his significance only when we cease to worry about such questions. Our interest in the events of his life, and above all in the cross, is more than an academic concern with the history of the past. We can see meaning in them only when we ask what God is trying to say to each one of us through them. Again, the figure of Jesus cannot be understood simply from his inner-worldly context. In mythological language, this means that he stems from eternity, his origin is not a human and natural one.

We shall not, however, pursue the examination of the particular incident of his life any further. In the end the crux of the matter lies in the cross and resurrection.[35]

As can be seen, for Bultmann kerygma is at the level of a historical absolute, perhaps in the spirit of Hegel's "Absolute Idea." In the first century, Paul, of course, announced that *the* eschatological event put an end to history as the mere unfolding or occurrence of a chronicle of happenings, i.e., the "Kingdom of God transcends the historical order."

What such thought appears to proclaim is that meaning is to be sought in "incidents" which transcend history, i.e., love and forgiveness as a force directed toward *me*.[36] That meaning does not come from the life of Jesus as a figure of past history, that is a life demonstrable by historical research,[37] but rather from an unclouded eye (the eye of faith) that can see the action(s) of God that the usual worldly events shroud and obscure.[38] Presumably, these "incidents" are available to all who crucify their old nature of "passions and desires" as *The Letter of Paul to the Galatians* 5:24 declares. To Bultmann, passions and desires seem to include the desire for knowledge and truth as a form of security that interferes with pristine "trust in the Lord."[39]

Two claims are being made that Bultmann has characterized as paradox. Paradox is not a mitigating factor; it is a complicating one. What sacrifice is being demanded in the following?

> Jesus Christ is certainly presented as the son of God, a preexistent divine being, and therefore to that extent a mythical figure. But he is also a concrete figure of history—Jesus of Nazareth. His life is more than a mythical event; it is a human life which ended in the tragedy of crucifixion. We have here a unique combination of history and myth.[40]

Not only is the combination unique, but the explanation is also:

> The paradox is just this, that a human figure, Jesus of Nazareth . . . with a recognizable place in world history, and therefore exposed to the objective observation of the historian and intelligible within their context in world history—are not thus apprehended and understood as what they really are, namely as the act of God, as *the* eschatological event.[41]

Truly did Bultmann declare that kerygma is a dehistoricizing view. If an extraordinary spiritual existence was made into a physical fact, it has to be demonstrated and apprehended as physical fact; one may not shrink from the consequence of not meeting those requirements. Thus, it does not suffice to speak of deeper symbolic meaning or to offer sanctification under the characterization "kerygmatic certainty." A pragmatic test applied to a pluralism of religiously satisfying divinities becomes a dangerous two-edged blade.

The positing of a spiritual existence in kerygmatic certainty is also characteristic of the work of Albert Schweitzer. The "quest" in his daring and monumental work, *The Quest of the Historical Jesus,* was held by him to be hopeless and irrelevant. One hundred and fifty years of laborious and searching effort came to naught, for the writings about a Jesus were not intended to provide a "Life of Jeus," but kerygmatically to proclaim his words and actions as God's revelation and salvation. Apparently, Schweitzer also shrank back from the findings of his own investigation. Ascension, apotheosis, and removal from the earth seemed to be the right path; celestially, a figure becomes unassailable. Thus,

There is nothing more negative than the result of the critical study of the life of Jesus. The Jesus of Nazareth who came forward publicly as the messiah, who preached the ethic of the Kingdom of God, who founded the Kingdom of Heaven upon earth and died to give his work its final consecration, never had any existence. He is a figure designed by rationalism, endowed with life by liberalism, and clothed by modern theology in an historical garb.[42]

Schweitzer brings his magnificent work to a close with an homiletical version of the mystical plea of *Mara Na Tha,* (Lord, Please Come!). He consoles us that His Kingdom *will* come, i.e., we can redeem ourselves if we carry within us hope of the Kingdom of God.

The abiding and eternal in Jesus is absolutely independent of historical knowledge and can only be understood by contact with His spirit which is still at work in the world. In proportion as we have the spirit of Jesus we have the true knowledge of Jesus.[43]

Some of the "Lives of Jesus" presented and analyzed within Schweitzer's work clearly deny the historicity of gospel writings and then proceed to paint a life based on the gospel portrait. This is true of Schweitzer and Bultmann as well; it seems as if they believe the spirit (if not the letter) of gospel writings is correct. Whether one is a strict unitarian or a committed iconoclast, somehow an abiding reverence is reflected even in the humble assertion that Jesus is *only* a man (and not a divine incarnation). What is it that lies behind the "only"? *What* a man! The supreme man of all history, Schweitzer's Ideal Man! What emerges from its concealment, or even denial, is that the essence of religious thought is found in the *story* of Jesus, his perforation and penetration into the world scene: the *only* difference between an "ordinary" Jesus and the rest of humanity is his divinity. The real paradox is that conviction is considered as demonstration of either divinity or humanity, distinctions between them being seen only as aspects of the same substance.

A faith that dares to make a transcendent God immanent on the earth cannot escape a historical test through appeal to argument and logic, but is able to elude it through tacit belief portrayed as methodological medium. Classic Judaic belief avoided the problem in its insistence on a purely mental construction and negative conception of God, i.e., pure and abiding transcendence, never to be apprehended by the senses. The theory of kerygmatic certainty of Bultmann (and Paul) is a powerful tool; it offers the renewability of certitude. Doubt is easy, a natural state; it is conviction that is difficult and requires continual reaffirmation.

Unlike an earlier, incomplete testament recording the foibles, shortcomings, and failures of a frail humanity, the later testament is a tale of perfection within a singularly fulfilled existence. Creativity is neither needed nor desired to make *it* more complete. One event (if one may use that temporal term) is the most spectacular; we are kerygmatically certain that it cannot be equalled by correspondence with any other event, let alone duplicated. Nevertheless, our human weakness gives rise to doubt, the enemy of certainty, and that doubt requests certification of a story. The certification comes in the form of a renewal of the image of completion and fulfillment (the old ontological proof of Anselm.) In Schweitzer's words, the Kingdom of God is already here in our midst and has only to be acknowledged as the fullness of time (the eschaton). An Overman has been given us and all that needs to be done is to adore him and exult in him. Indeed, a Billy Graham would assure us the enjoyment of everlasting life if we but affirm: "I believe that He died for me." Not only does he wash us clean (of sin) so that we feel as newly reborn, but he gives substance to our understanding of "the good" by personifying it.

The idea of kerygma and kerygmatic certainty may be applied, however imperfectly, to a secular setting that may be useful in its being comprehended. "All men are created equal" is an article of faith easily recognized. As expression of a normative belief in fair treatment, a social group can strive to implement it, even though it will inevitably fall short of its objective. One of the reasons therefor is not a failure of will or intent, but because the statement asserts an empirical falsehood. It is simply not a statement of palpable fact; the fact is rather the opposite! The faith that is being expressed, however, is that there is intention to *strive* to achieve *some idea* of equality. Yet, there are some who become bedeviled into believing that the assertion itself proclaims something that *is* demonstrable. If we hold with kerygma theology that a Jesus is *outside* history and its continuities, an investigation into written records for a historical person is then fruitless. By the same token, original communities of believers, as well as the centralized Church of 325 C.E., were claimants to, *not* witnesses of, nonhistorical phenomena. Similar to the assertion in the Declaration of Independence, certain claims in the New Testament were reflections of kerygma: proclamations of commitment to some idea(l) to be realized. The question that remains unanswerable is: Can personal truth substitute for publicly available truth(s)? *Pace* Kierkegaard!

The Parable of Compensation

Psychological theory explains the source of collective fantasy as a response to disappointment and frustration of hopes and desires, especially of those that are unquenchable. An expectation, in fantasy, inexorably breeds disappointment and frustration. As collective disappointments and intense frustrations continue in experience, the fantasy structure becomes stronger in heightened expectation; the vision grows in proportion to the pain endured. Thus, a repeating cycle, set in motion, ultimately explodes. The form of the explosion can result in creativity, as in a new style of art, poetry, and philosophy; it is also destructive in that an old order gets swept away.

Study of Near-Eastern thought in the two-century period from 50 B.C.E. to 150 C.E. reveals its tremulous and convulsive nature. Huge collective visions floated aloft, alongside massive ground-level experiences of disappointment below. Tales and theories of cosmic redemption were in heavy demand, a demand fueled daily by new experiences of suffering. Any political expression of liberty and sovereignty was ruthlessly suppressed or quickly throttled, even as messianic promises of purely political restoration of national fortunes multiplied, alongside otherworldly apocalyptic pronouncements. In the Near-Eastern provinces under Roman domination, social inequalities were sharp and bristling as the imperial civil service fattened itself on the exploitation of subject peoples. In Judaea as elsewhere, the characteristic pattern revealed a huge pyramidal structure, with the lowest stratum consisting of debt slaves who had suffered uprooting from the land. (As was customary then [and now], taxation from above was passed along until it reached the bottom layer of society.) The rural peasantry, then, often turned to brigandage as the only means of economic pursuit, or it joined with a rootless urban proletariat in day-to-day hire, and in class resentment and hostility against the merchants or commercial groups of the cities. Resentment was directed at each higher stratum on the pyramidal structure by the group(s) below it. Toward the narrower apex, hatred was aimed at the rich in general, while for the rulership class at the very point of the pyramid (the foreign power and its servile sycophants) there was the vision of apocalyptic overturn. A day of reckoning was coming when equality would reign supreme. An impression of the milieu of social hostility may be received from the following excerpt of *A Letter of James,* 5:1–5:

> Next a word to you who are rich. Weep and wail over the miserable
> fate overtaking you.

Your riches have rotted away; your fine clothes are moth-eaten;
    your silver and gold have corroded, and their corrosion will
    be evidence against you and consume your flesh like fire.
You have piled up wealth in an age that is near its close.
The wages you never paid to the men who mowed your fields
    are crying aloud against you, and the outcry of the reapers has
    reached the ears of the Lord of Hosts.
You have lived on the land in wanton luxury, gorging yourselves—
    and that on the day appointed for your slaughter.

Such imprecations and open expressions of promiscuous hatred pro-
liferated and were aimed within as well as without: the country-dweller
against the city resident, the unschooled versus the educated, the terrorist
"dagger-men" (whom Josephus called the Sicarii) against the symbols of
Roman authority. However, the *form* of the hatred among the tormented
and the despairing was distinguishable, even if it appeared as a unity.
Apocalyptists hated in fantasy and imagination; zealots (as they came to
be known) hated in political and military skirmish with an oppressive authority. Even so, religiously-clothed messages of complete overturn—where
the poor would be rich, the hungry satisfied, and the oppressed mighty—
contributed to a chiliastic atmosphere, saturated with the expectancy and
eschatological fervor, that "the end" was coming.

In *The Gospel According to Luke,* a message of unmistakable revolution is put forth in the retrojections of a later generation (6:20–25):

Blessed are you who are in need; the Kingdom of God is yours.
Blessed are you who now go hungry; you will be satisfied.
Blessed are you who weep now; you will laugh. . . .
But alas for you who are rich; you have had your time of happiness.
Alas for you who are well-fed now; you will go hungry.
Alas for you who laugh now; you will mourn and weep.

While periodic tremors of violence shook the country of Judaea reg-
ularly and continued to accelerate from 37 B.C.E. on, that is, with the
accession of Herod as puppet ruler, massive explosion occurred in the
reign of the Emperor Nero in 65 C.E. The national misfortune was then
projected on to a cosmic screen, taking place not on earth, but in the
heavens above. In the year 70, a catastrophe of epic proportions occurred:
the House of God, and the city of God, went up in flames as the attempt
to throw off the Roman yoke was smashed. The convulsion shook the
foundation of a world faith and it was never again the same. On the
cosmic screen, crucifixion—a daily spectacle in the siege of Jerusalem[44]—
was *not* the end. (Josephus describes how an open display of whipping,

tormenting, and finally crucifixion [i.e., all three in sequence] was part of a deliberate Roman policy to weaken the will of defenders of the city. He lists a figure of five hundred a day; this was probably the accounting of an unusual occurrence, the capture of the desperate and starving who attempted to escape the besieged city.) The tormented and humiliated would be elevated to sit at God's "right hand," and God would adopt him as his own son. Fevered imagination—unchained by the shock and fury of a war of total annihilation—roamed freely in projection, personification, and identification with the image of a Redeemer. The free-floating material of the ages had washed ashore.

It is well to record the aftermath:

(1) The overthrow of a Temple cultus and priestly hierarchy created a political-religious void into which a new structure—a loose confederation of existing associations and brotherhoods (and a nascent provincial synagogue)—claimed legitimacy of succession.

(2) The annihilation of a national polity and reduction of national will into submission, passivity, and withdrawal. However, the memory of an aggressive policy of proselytization—that had been entrenched within the far reaches of the Empire—did not expire.

(3) Dispersion of official Judaic ideas: messianism or a congeries of hopes, salvation in a future life, and their intermixture with Hellenistic rituals and myths.

(4) Amid the vision of a heavenly Jerusalem replacing the earthly one, and with the projection of a picture of overthrow of secular kingdoms and the introduction of a kingdom ruled by God (Daniel 7:17–27), the Judaic canon of sacred writings was held as a primary documentary source, and as evidentiary basis for a revised edition— the *new* testament.

*   *   *

With the Temple gone, the daily offering to God was ended and the mournful lamentation of the bereft could be heard: "How can we now worship? God's glory has departed." Some other voices proclaimed: "God is now here on earth. A replacement sacrifice has been prepared in which you can partake."

So began the Christian era.

Notes

Cultural Prepossession

1. Scant references in the Talmud are not contemporaneous accounts; such late and oblique references as do occur reflect circulating Christian teachings. Of more than fifteen thousand pages in the Talmud, only thirty-six contain a passage that deals with Judaeo-Christians and other sects and their opinions. There are only two explicit references to the messiah in the sixty-four tractates of the twelve-hundred pages of the Mishna (compiled in 200 C.E.): "footsteps of the messiah" and "the messianic age."

2. Cited in Edgar J. Goodspeed, *The Apostolic Fathers* (New York: Harper and Brothers, 1950), Fragment 2, #4, p. 265. Translation based on the Funk-Bihlmeyer edition, vol. 2, published at Tübingen, 1924.

3. John M. Robertson, *Christianity and Mythology* (London: Watts and Company, 1900), p. 431.

Geographical Locations

4. C. Raymond Beazley, *The Dawn of Modern Geography,* vol. 1 (Oxford: The Clarendon Press, 1897; reprinted 1949), p. 281.

5. M. Avi-Yonah and Ehpraim Stern, *Encyclopaedia of Archaeological Excavations in the Holy Land,* vol. 3 (Jerusalem: The Israel Exploration Society and Massada Press, 1977), p. 919.

6. George Adam Smith, *Historical Geography of the Holy Land* (New York: Hodder and Stoughton, 1896), p. 432.

7. George Adam Smith, *Jerusalem: Topography, Economics, and History from the Earliest Times to A.D. 70* (Library of Biblical Studies, 1877; reprint, Keter Publishing House, 1972).

8. Avi-Yonah and Stern; p. 919.

9. Ibid.

10. Michael Avi-Yonah, *The Jews of Palestine: A Political History from the Bar Kokhba War to the Arab Conquest* (Oxford: Basil Blackwell, 1976), pp. 138–39.

11. Gonzalo Báez-Camargo, *Archaeological Commentary on the Bible* (Garden City, N.Y.: Doubleday and Company, 1986), pp. 220–21.

12. James H. Charlesworth, *Jesus Within Judaism: New Light from Exciting Archaeological Discoveries,* The Anchor Bible Reference Library (New York: Doubleday, 1988), pp. 111, 109.

13. Eusebius, *Life of Constantine,* III: 41–43, cited in Jack Finegan, *Light from the Ancient Past* (Princeton University Press, 1946), p. 438.

14. That piety located sites is well illustrated by the *Via Dolorosa* or Way of Sorrows, described as "the way on which Christ walked carrying the Cross"

(whereon "Stations of the Cross" were identified). The *way* was first reported in 1294 C.E. by the pilgrim, Friar Ricoldus de Monte Crucis. J. C. M. Laurent, *Peregrinatores Medii Aevi Quatuor,* 2d ed. (1873) cited in Finegan, p. 242.

15. Allen Godbey, *The Lost Tribes A Myth* (Durham, N.C.: Duke University Press, 1930), p. 71.

16. Colm Luibhéid, *The Essential Eusebius* (New York: The New American Library, 1966), pp. 201–205.

17. *Itinerarium Hierosolymitanum.* About the Jerusalem Itinerary.

18. F. Tozer, *A History of Ancient Geography,* Cambridge Geographical Series (Cambridge University Press, 1897; reprinted New York: Biblo and Tannen, 1964), p. 309.

19. For example, the following Hebrew words and their cognate equivalents in Aramaic:

Hebrew		Aramaic
Nefesh	Life-Soul	Nafsha
Guf	Body	Gufa
Leḥem	Bread	Laḥma
Eved	Servant	Avda
Melekh	King	Malka
Olam	World	Olma
Igeret	Letter	Igarta
Galut	Exile	Galuta
Shabbat	Sabbath	Shabbeta
Malkhut	Kingdom	Malkhuta
Gulgolet	Skull	Gulgolta

The Error of Homologization

20. John Stuart Mill, "Theism," *Three Essays on Religion* (New York: Henry Holt, 1874), pp. 253–54.

21. The chronological effect created by mere *placement* of the Letters *after* gospel writings is *this* before *that.* Even in the writings of the noted Rudolf Bultmann one can discern its traces.

22. Edgar J. Goodspeed, *The Apostolic Fathers* (New York: Harper and Brothers, 1950), Fragment 2, #4, p. 265.

23. Samuel Sandmel, *We Jews and Jesus* (New York: Oxford University Press, 1969), p. 65.

24. R. Bultmann claims that ". . . Jesus actually lived as a Jewish rabbi," i.e., as a teacher. The subtitle of section 1 of chapter 3 in the following work is "Jesus as Rabbi," Rudolf Bultmann, *Jesus and the Word* (New York: Charles Scribner's Sons, 1958), pp. 57–61.

25. Bishop Albert Kalthoff speaks of the ideological current galvanizing the first-century socio-political milieu: "The crude social ferment in the Roman Empire amalgamated itself with the religious and philosophical forces of the time to form the new Christian social movement" [of messianic apocalypticism and communism among the oppressed masses] (Albert Schweitzer, *The Quest of the Historical Jesus* [New York: The Macmillan Company, 1948], p. 317).

26. William F. Albright, *From the Stone Age to Christianity* (Baltimore: The Johns Hopkins Press, 1946), pp. 307–308.

27. ". . . *Jesus Christ confronts man in the kerygma and nowhere else; just as he confronted Paul himself and forced him to the decision. The kerygma does not proclaim universal truths, or a timeless idea—whether it is an idea of God or of a redeemer—but a historical fact.*" (Rudolf Bultmann, *Faith and Understanding* [New York: Harper and Row Publishers, 1969], p. 241).

Kerygma Rather Than Historicity

28. ". . . the righteous will live by being faithful" (Habakkuk 2:4).

29. Heinz Zahrnt, *The Historical Jesus* (New York: Harper and Brothers, 1963), p. 85.

30. Rudolf Bultmann, *Jesus Christ and Mythology* (New York: Charles Scribner's Sons, 1958), p. 36.

31. Ibid., p. 81.

32. Ibid., pp. 79–80.

33. Rudolf Bultmann, *Kerygma and Myth* (New York: Harper and Row Publishers, 1966), p. 207.

34. Bultmann, *Faith and Understanding,* p. 30.

35. Bultmann, *Kerygma and Myth,* p. 35.

36. Rudolf Bultmann, *Faith and Understanding* (New York: Harper and Row Publishers, 1969), p. 38.

37. Bultmann, *Kerygma and Myth,* p. 38.

38. Bultmann, *Jesus Christ and Mythology,* pp. 61–62.

39. There is no difference between security based on good works and security built on objectifying knowledge. The man who desires to believe in God must know that he has nothing at his own disposal on which to build this faith, that he is, so to speak, in a vacuum. He who abandons every form of security shall find the true security. (Bultmann, *Jesus Christ and Mythology,* p. 84).

40. Bultmann, *Kerygma and Myth,* p. 34.

41. Ibid., p. 208.

42. Albert Schweitzer, *The Quest of the Historical Jesus* (New York: The Macmillan Company, 1948), p. 398.

43. Ibid., p. 401.

The Parable of Compensation

44. "So the soldiers . . . nailed those they caught one after one way, and another after another, to the crosses . . . when the multitude was so great, that room was wanting for the crosses, and crosses wanting for the bodies" (*War of the Jews,* Book V, 11:1 in *Josephus: Complete Works,* trans. William Whiston [Grand Rapids, Mich.: Kregel Publications, 1985], p. 565. See also V, 6:5).

4

And the Word Became Flesh

Introduction

To recapitulate salient points thus far, we do not know when the events presented in New Testament writings took place or even their exact location. The attempt to link them to a definite prefecture under a particular Imperial Legate is an ad hoc amendment, unsubstantiated independently and unsubstantiable. Gospels are the only authority for gospels. Since the writings are primarily a confession and affirmation of belief, it is difficult to differentiate between datum and dream, the real and the imagined. Traditions about salvation (*yeshua*) were themselves constraints on such writings; their effects could not be escaped, i.e., demonism and possession, end-of-the world prophecies, cosmic-redeemer myths. Given the huge multiform collection of ritual practices in the human war against a ubiquitous demonism, as well as the widespread diffusion of potions, treatments, and cures for possession by evil forces, amulets and tattooing being only one example (the modern drug store is an up-to-date version), it can be understood that end-of-the-world prophecies and cosmic-redeemer myths would be part of the ordnance to be stored in the religious armory for a life and death struggle. Who can catalogue the entire spectrum of multi-layered religious thoughts compressed within the single figure of a Jesus? The variety may be traced only in outline: mysterious birth and incarnation of a god, the "raising up" of a king, human sacrifice, exegesis of an older testament and casuistic resolution thereunto, universal dominion in a theocratic state. Interwoven are metaphysical doctrines such as atonement and purification of the sins of humanity, sinlessness, resurrection of the dead, sacramental meal of the deity. The coalescence of these elements and doctrines—perhaps the metaphor of *congealing* is more appropriate—over centuries results in a composite creation. By collective assent and spurred on by widespread demand, solidification occurs within a single conceptualization: salvation. The process of objectification constructs from that conceptualization—*yeshua*—a name, a recognized figure who walks the earth and who will succor it.

That such an idea possesses force and meaning to those already filled with conviction and fervent desire to believe and hope, its essential mystery eludes feeble attempts at characterization, let alone description. In this view, the momentary disturbance that Nazareth and Golgotha derive from nomenclature rather than topography emanates from a preoccupation with temporality and human categories of knowledge, all unimportant in the face of the enduring and timeless. As *The Gospel According to John* (8:23) puts it: "Jesus continued, 'You belong to this world below, I to the world above. Your home is in this world, mine is not.' " This concept of the enduring and timeless is central and critical to the rise of the movement that became Christianity.

The "enduring and the timeless" also includes legend, thus, in order to believe we have to disbelieve. It is assumed that few would have difficulty in characterizing the story of Salome and the Dance of the Seven Veils as legend, i.e., the ornamentation and embellishment of a tale around a semi-historical figure. As first presented in gospel writings, it makes for a good story.

The Characteristics of a Good Story

> It was this Herod [Antipas] who sent men to arrest John [the Baptist] and put him in prison at the instance of his brother Philip's wife, Herodias, whom he had married. John had told him, "You have no right to take your brother's wife." Herodias nursed a grudge against John and would willingly have killed him, but she could not, for Herod went in awe of him, knowing him to be a good and holy man; so he gave him his protection. He liked to listen to him, although what he heard left him greatly disturbed.
>
> Herodias found her opportunity when Herod on his birthday gave a banquet to his chief officials and commanders and the leading men of Galilee. Her daughter came in and danced, and so delighted Herod and his guests that the king said to the girl, "Ask me for anything you like and I will give it to you." He even said on oath: "Whatever you ask I will give you, up to half my kingdom." She went out and said to her mother, "What shall I ask for?" She replied, "The head of John the Baptist!" The girl hurried straight back to the king with her request: "I want you to give me, here and now, on a dish, the head of John

the Baptist." The king was greatly distressed, yet because of his oath and his guests he could not bring himself to refuse her. He sent a soldier of the guard with orders to bring John's head; and the soldier went to the prison and beheaded him; then he brought the head on a dish, and gave it to the girl; and she gave it to her mother.

When John's disciples heard the news, they came and took his body away and laid it in a tomb. (*The Gospel According to Mark* 6:17–29)

The tale holds our attention and interest with plot, theme, action, and grisly climax, and it does not matter whether or not it happened; it *sounds* good. The version presented in *The Gospel According to Matthew* 14:1–12 is not quite as "good." The story has been further enriched by Oscar Wilde and adorned musically by Richard Strauss to imprint Salome and her Seven Veils on our minds.

In Josephus XVIII 5:2, the above incident reads as follows:

Herod [Antipas], who feared lest the great influence John had over the people might put it in his power and inclination to raise a rebellion (for they seemed ready to do anything he should advise) thought it best, by putting him to death, to prevent any mischief he might cause, and not bring himself into difficulties, by sparing a man who might make him repent of it when it should be too late. Accordingly he was sent a prisoner, out of Herod's suspicious temper, to Macherus, the castle I before mentioned, and was there put to death.

Further on, in chapter 5:4, Josephus presents some genealogical material:

Herodias, their sister, was married to Herod [Philip], the son of Herod the Great, who was born of Mariamne, the daughter of Simon the high priest, who had a daughter Salome; after whose birth, Herodias took upon her to confound the laws of our country, and divorce herself from her husband, while he was alive, and was married to Herod [Antipas] her husband's brother by the father's side. . . .

The latter account seems arid and devoid of "human interest" (gossip and scandal) material. Not many would have difficulty in identifying it as reportorial, the dominant style of the journalist or chronicler. The differences between the accounts in Mark and Josephus are not limited to style alone. In Josephus, there is no banquet, no dancing girl, and no request for the head of John on a dish or otherwise, while these particulars abound in the Marcan version. (One is reminded of the ease of improvisatory dance movements wherein the dancer is only concerned with self-expression.) Disagreement on the place of execution and on the motive for execution is apparent.

The similarities between the two accounts lie in identification of the names of the principals, with one notable exception: the name Salome, which appears only in Josephus; in Mark and Matthew, the only reference is to a daughter of Herodias. There is also agreement on the violation of a nation's marriage laws by two of the principals and on an execution of a prisoner. One might conclude that there is some agreement on the bare facts, but on the interpretation of those facts, there is disparity. Do the bare facts speak? At best, they provide a basis for concluding that certain individuals existed at a certain location. The significance of the execution is a matter of reasoned conjecture: were the reasons therefore pure retaliatory malice (Herodias), fear of political/religious consequences (Herod Antipas), or a combination of these? It is obvious that, in the absence of other data, inferences have to be limited.

What is abundantly clear in the tale told in chapter 6 of Mark is the release of imagination into the atmosphere. Romance and lore fly freely, and when an Oscar Wilde and a Richard Strauss give expression to the millennial fancy, its historicity becomes assured. The following is an excerpt from a review of a production of *Salome:* "Salome is certainly a challenging role for a Broadway debut. The Old Testament princess who performed the Dance of the Seven Veils for Herod and then demanded, and got, the head of John the Baptist . . . is often considered a biblical bimbo."[1] The references to the Bible (whether Old or New Testament) is, of course, diaphanous error, but what is fascinating is how human fancy and imaginative flight, over a millennial span, come to be knowledge-forms.

The Misconstrual of Allegory

Sometimes legend fuses with allegory or parable where there is an overt attempt to teach "something else." For instance, in the story of Cain and Abel, the main purpose seems to be to highlight moral teaching rather than to present an actual historical occurrence between two individuals; in this case, a prohibition against wanton murder. The historical developments suggested by the story may be viewed through the theoretical construct of a clash between economic interests: that of the pastoral herder-nomad and that of the settler-farmer, and it may also provide insight into the necessity for historical sanctions against wanton murder, and the nature of those sanctions, i.e., the use of strong tabus (e.g., blood pollutes the land). Such a construct would obviously have greater explanatory power, but it might be less appealing because a human element had been extracted from it. Nevertheless, the very elements which make the tale appealing transport along with them the likelihood of distortion and misconstrual, as well as misapplication. Most religious didacticism of the Cain and Abel (or Jacob and Esau) variety, is set forth in the *individualization* of what usually is part of a *collective* phenomenon or development. For instance, what has been referred to as the "Stolen Blessing" in the story of Jacob and Esau may be seen as an ongoing institutional struggle between theories of inheritance. Was the ages-old practice of ultimogeniture (born of a matriarchal organization of society) to continue or was primogeniture (the new organization) to prevail? Thus, it is not infrequently that moral teaching is mistaken for historical event(s) by a massive transportation. *Individualization* is well-suited for moral teaching; it is ill-suited as socio-historical explanation. That it gets adapted (distorted might be more appropriate) to the latter purpose is a feature of the human tendency to identification, anthropomorphization, and to the endowing of ideas with materiality.

In an age of science, few have difficulty with the recognition of myth—so long as it is not *our* myth. The endowment of an idea with life or materiality is readily apprehended in the case of Aphrodite or Venus, which appealingly makes a more agreeable impression on us than the mental construct "sexual energy" does. The great effusion of art in *her* honor is testimony to that impression. So it is not strange to encounter a straightforward presentation of Heracles by Diodorus Siculus, the Sicilian historian of the first century B.C.E., as if Heracles were an actual historical being, to wit: Heracles was the great-grandson of Perseus, son of Zeus and Danae. Heracles' mother, Alcmene, was impregnated by Zeus also, hence Heracles' claim to immortality.[2] That fictional characters in romance sometimes have acquired life through the agency of human thought is not difficult to demonstrate.

Earlier, it was said that in order to believe we have to disbelieve. The *process* of doubting entails tolerance of insecurity. It means the release of a possession which is familiar and treasured. If the particular possession has been with us a long time, its loss becomes very difficult to bear; each day is a reexperience of bereavement. Thus, in fearing the consequences of doubting, we bring doubt *itself* to bear on the process of doubting, the inchoate argument being expressed in the state of disbelief: "How could such a story be invented?" The rhetorical question makes clear that "invention" is typically conceived as a momentary, spontaneous, individualized flash out of a "nothingness" rather than the cumulative process of a slow, glacial-like millennial development. Ultimately, the invention-doubter's argument rests on the existence of a body of believers to whom credibility is ascribed for the canonization of a christ-ist theory, as the best possible explanation for the union between heaven and earth.

The clothing of an idea in human form takes many shapes. We turn now to human inventiveness of the *idea* of idea itself, and the forms in which it was expressed and presented.

The Idea of Idea

The Influence of Plato (427–347 B.C.E.). This original thinker had a profound effect on humanity across centuries. The beauty of his conceptions and their expression often made them compelling and, indeed, many have mistaken this aesthetic quality for actuality and truth. Plato was concerned with the relationship of the universal to the particular, and claimed that universals have an existence prior to, and as patterns determining the nature of, the individual particulars that compose the universal. Thus, a *particular* tree partakes of the *universal* quality of tree-ness. Plato believed that universals actually exist in a nontemporal, nonspatial realm, independent of the space-time world which mortals occupy. These universals were called by him Ideas or Forms. Although the forms are nowhere to be found in the empirical world (e.g., a perfect circle) since they exist apart from sense experience, we can give expression to them and recreate them; *that* is proof of their reality.

Moreover, in their invisibility they provide us with understanding, for as Plato put it in his allegory of the cave, the visible world is one of *appearance* only. What is visible is unintelligible; it is the invisible world that *is* intelligible, that provides clarity and understanding. (In contemporary terms, the theoretical nonexistent explains what it is that we view.)

Ecclesiasticus. Within two centuries—due in no small measure to the conquests of Alexander the Great—Plato's ideas had become influential and had been diffused widely, although dramatically altered in *shape,* ultimately to become materialized. Circa 180 B.C.E., the *Book of Ecclesiasticus* or the *Wisdom of Yeshua* [Jesus] *ben Sirah* appeared in Jerusalem, testimony to the spread of Hellenism. It is classified as one of the Hidden Books (Apocrypha) although much is known about the date and personality of the author (which is not true of other Apocryphal works). The work is less a religious tract than one of social-civic conduct and matters worldly, although its opening verse declares: "All wisdom comes from the Lord and remains with him forever." Its style employs the use of couplets, perhaps suited to proverbs or sayings, as indicated in the following:

For wisdom is what her name implies
And to most men she is invisible.
Listen, my child, and accept my opinion,
And do not refuse my advice.
Put your feet into her fetters,
And your neck into her collar.
Put your shoulder under her and carry her,
And do not weary of her chains;
Come to her with all your heart,
And follow her ways with all your might.
Inquire and search, and she will be made known to you,
And when you have grasped her, do not let her go.
For at last you will find the rest she gives,
And you will find her turning into gladness.[3]

This is easily recognized as figurative language and some may even find it difficult to translate into practical pursuit. Yet, one can note in the suggestion of visual imagery something that can almost be touched and held. If wisdom were to be conceived as a historical person, that would certainly erase its distance and unapproachability. In the following selection, wisdom is made to speak:

Come to me you who desire me
And fill yourselves with my produce.
For the memory of me is sweeter than honey,
And the possession of me, than the honeycomb.
Those who eat me will still be hungry,
And those who drink me will still be thirsty.
He who obeys me will not be put to shame,
And those who work with me will commit no sin.[4]

Now, can we imagine sleep as a mythical figure, speaking in the following way?

Come to me, all who are weary and whose load is heavy;
I will give you rest.
Take my yoke upon you, and learn from me,
for I am gentle and humble-hearted; and you will find
rest for your souls.
For my yoke is easy to wear, my load is light.

The message might actually soothe us enough to enter into embrace with Morpheus. If one were to ask which of the above selections requires an actual person, the response might be that both selections can be received as figurative without any difficulty. The first is typically seen as *pure* idea while the second—written much later—was ascribed to a person possessing existence (*The Gospel According to Matthew* 11:28–30).

Traces of the thought of Ben Sirah, taken as common knowledge, may be found in gospel writings. For instance, Ecclesiasticus 28:2 reads: "Forgive your neighbor his wrongdoing; then your sins will be forgiven you when you pray." The verse in Matthew 6:14 declares: "For if you forgive others the wrongs they have done, your heavenly Father will also forgive you," while Mark 11:25 reads: "And when you stand praying, if you have a grievance against anyone, forgive him, so that your Father in heaven may forgive you the wrongs you have done." Such expressions were held in a common storehouse, open to appropriation by all.

The Wisdom of Solomon. Another didactic book (part of the Hidden Books series, known as Wisdom Literature) appeared in Alexandria in the first century B.C.E. It represents a fusion of Greek and Judaic ideas and its author(s) is unknown, Solomon's name being employed for associative prestige and reflected honor. Wisdom is presented as a divine being, identified with the divine spirit, present at the creation of the world:

> For when gentle silence enveloped everything,
> And night was midway of her swift course,
> Your all-powerful word leaped from heaven, from the royal throne,
> A stern warrior, into the midst of the doomed land,
> Carrying for a sharp sword your undisguised command,
> And stood still and filled all things with death,
> And touched heaven but walked upon the earth.[5]

> For wisdom is more mobile than any motion
> And she penetrates and permeates everything
>   because she is so pure;
> For she is the breath of the power of God,
> And a pure emanation of his almighty glory;
> Therefore nothing defiled can enter into her . . .
> When I considered these things with myself,
> And reflected in my mind
> That in kinship with wisdom there is immortality. . . .[6]

In these excerpts, one can begin to see that a construct or conceptualization can be endowed with substance by the mere release of the energy of thought upon it. Technically, this is called hypostatization, or more popularly, personification. Sometimes we forget that what we have invented has no real substance beyond the construction that our thoughts have fashioned, and thus, we begin to "thingify," to speak of "*the* market" (of finance and investments) as if it possessed substantiality. Indeed, the United States Supreme Court has ruled that a corporation is a *Person.* As a legal principle with severely circumscribed implications, the ruling can be understood even literally; detached from the legal context and applied freely, an enormous delusive snare awaits. As Ecclesiasticus reminds us: "For many have been led astray by their imagination, and a wicked fancy has made our minds slip" (3:24). An illustration of the ready tendency of hypostatization or the substantialization of a concept is found in the folktale of the Polish rustic who declared how happy he was now that Poland had regained its sovereignty from Russian domination, because he was "no longer able to endure those terrible 'Russian' winters." His companion rejoined with: "Winter is not all that long. January, February, March—and 'before you know it,' it's spring!"

Philo of Alexandria. Thus far, we have noted the development of idea-personification, the encasing of thought within a human form. By the first century C.E., after two hundred years of theosophical speculation and the appearance of the Hidden Books, the full flower had begun to unfold: Divine Wisdom produced the world, and *Sophia* walked about the earth *as* a person. It was not that an actual person became more deified, rather, it was that an abstraction became more and more personified. Plato's thought "found" a chief expositor in Philo (Philon) (20 B.C.E.–ca. 50 C.E.), who was referred to as "Plato of the Jews." A well-known saying returned the compliment, referring to Plato as simply Moses, atticizing. Philo's writings were to become very influential, synthesizing Iranian, Hellenistic, and Judaic thought within the schema of a Logos concept ("Word"). That concept was to be invested with full humanity, so that the term "personification" no longer suffices to explain what was to transpire. (Incidentally, the precise relationship between Sophia and Logos is a complex, mystical weave, better left to specialized study of Gnostic thought.) In addition to the broadcasting of a Logos "idea," Philo's hermeneutical method, the allegory—the extraction of the spiritual rather then the literal significance—came to dominate the art of exegetical interpretation of Scripture. To Philo, the concept of Logos offered an explanation of the attainment of divine insight by the enlightened members of the Gentile world, who had not been privileged to experience a Sinaitic revelation. At the same time, a Logos "idea" together with the Greek Septuagint version of Scriptures offered the prospect of an active proselytizing program. This program was to pave a smoother roadway for later missionaries who were preaching a Pauline theological vision.

Now, how does one describe an incremental process of personification of a Logos "idea"? Apotheosis and deification of an existing being (as was the case with Roman emperors, where an eagle was released over a funeral pyre to indicate ascension into heaven), was qualitatively distinct from what was taking place with Logos, as it slowly was fashioned into *the* Logos (or *the* Word). To state that it was the substantialization of an abstraction—the expression of a *form,* in Platonic terms—merely reports the *result* of the process; it is similar to describing the difference between an indefinite article (*a*) and a definite article (*the*). What happened to change *a* into *the*? An existence was brought into being to house an idea, as if to prevent its "wandering off," and it became the task, then, to cull a structure of incidents from already existing materials, preserved by confraternities and associations existing outside mainstream and institutional structures. Groups such as the Jesseans (probably interchangeable with Essenes, since the word is not found in any vernacular outside Greek) were repositories of collected incidents and events, providing the encasement structure to contain the "idea."

By the middle of the second century C.E., the opening declaration of *The Gospel According to John* revealed the fruits of several generations of theosophical speculation on Plato's universals or *forms* and Philo's Logos: "In the beginning was the Word [Logos], and the Word was with God, and the Word was God" (John 1:1). In Platonic terms, the very pronouncement—itself almost a hypostatization—extends beyond any *particular* incident or time period, since it is both before *and* after; it is dispatched into a state of timeless being, into the Platonic realm of preexistent Forms. It transcends history because it is beyond corporeality, i.e., beyond proofs that can be derived from the inferior empirical senses. At one and the same time, *the* Logos (or Form) can be expressed within a person of flesh and blood. The latter interpretation represented the culmination of a struggle between spiritualists and materialists or literalists. At this point, it is necessary to speak of the Gnostic influence that illumines the whole question of corporeality.

Gnostic Spirit. As has been observed in the Apocryphal work of Jewish Gnostics, *The Wisdom of Solomon,* divine wisdom was the original source material or substance of the world itself and it also came to be viewed as the basis of its redemption from sin and destruction. However, the origin of Gnostic thought—a seeking beneath the letter—was probably Iran, within the brotherhood known as Mandaean. *Manda,* signifying *Gnosis* or "Wisdom," involved the method of allegory, looking for deeper meaning than the apparent, or, in Paul's words, "the spirit." The intersection of Iranian, Judaic, and Hellenic ideas—that a pure spirit or idea exists in the Cosmos which infuses all of *matter* with its spiritual substance—

probably occurred at the world cultural capital of Alexandria. That infusion of spirit, or knowledge itself, is sufficient to direct the world on its course:

> He [the Gnostic] does not know because he has gradually learned; he knows because revelation has been given him. He does not believe, for faith is inferior to gnosis. And his gnosis . . . is itself perfect redemption. . . . For Gnostics know that they were originally spiritual beings who have come to live in souls and bodies; they once dwelt in the spiritual world above but have been made to fall into this world of sense and sin. Now, thanks to their self-knowledge, they are hastening back above, having been redeemed from this world below.[7]

The Gnostics (or "Knowers") held firmly to a conviction in the transcendence of God and to a purely spiritual nature, so much so that they came to identify *any* corporeality as essentially the product of sinfulness. For instance, a good God could not have created a corrupt and sinful world; that was the work of an inferior deity, a chief Archon or artisan god who controlled seven spirits dwelling between earth and heaven. A hint of this influence is suggested in 2 Corinthians 11:4 where it appears that *other* Jesuses were being proclaimed: A Messiah Jesus and a Logos Jesus. This statement also reflects a developing internal conflict within the movement itself. The declaration in *The Gospel According to John* 1:14, "So the Word became flesh," i.e., that an idea became a real existent, produced a collision between what emerged as a camp of materialists and a camp of spiritualists. For those who saw flesh as corruption and spirit as pure, what else could such an announcement be other than a battle cry that God could be *seen*?

First, for the materialist who insists on a representative in-the-flesh who resides on earth, a critical problem was made manifest. By what means could the flesh be dispatched back to the timeless and enduring realm from whence it had emanated? A response involved adoption of the Passion story as a sacred drama of glorification and exaltation, and the adaptation of the sacred meal of a mystery cult in which the absorption of the god defended the body against evil spirits. The resolution appears in *The Gospel According to John* 6:53–56:

> In every truth I tell you, unless you eat the flesh of the Son of Man and drink his blood you can have no life in you. Whoever eats my flesh and drinks my blood has eternal life and I will raise him up on the last day. . . . Whoever eats my flesh and drinks my blood dwells in me and I in him.

In verse 59, John also claims that these things—a theory of theophagy, to release the qualities of God—were expounded at the synagogue in Capernaum! (See p. 121.) If so, it would not be endearing to those in attendance any more so than it was to the disciples who were said to have exclaimed:

> This is more than we can stand! How can anyone listen to such talk? Jesus was aware that his disciples were grumbling about it and asked them, "Does this shock you?" . . . From that moment, many of his disciples drew back and no longer went with him. (John 6:60–66)

A Gnostic would have been shocked too, particularly the sect of Docetists (Dokein)[8] who held that Jesus was a psychic phenomenon who only "seemed" to suffer. This was an extreme form of Gnostic teaching that scorned everything physical, material substance being unable to receive salvation. As rigid dualists, Doc[k]etists spurned the "testimonies" (gospels) presented in support of an earthly Jesus, since he only "seemed" to have a real body.[9] For, "sharing the human lot" meant pain, involving a compromise of perfection as well as change in form; hence Jesus was only an apparent manifestation, a phantasm with a phantom body who lived on earth.

Needless to say, issues between spiritualists and materialists were to intensify. The verse in *The Second Letter of Paul to the Corinthians* 5:21 could be interpreted either in a spiritual or material sense: ". . . for our sake God made him one with human sinfulness, so that in him we might be made one with the righteousness of God." Yet, in *The Letter of Paul to the Philippians* 2:7–8, there seems to be an embrace and envelopment of both positions: "Bearing the human likeness, sharing the human lot, he humbled himself, and was obedient to the point of death." "Bearing the human likeness" suggests the "seeming" idea of Docetism; "sharing the human lot" suggests its opposite, *in the flesh*. (The revealed ambiguity may explain why such as Tertullian considered Paul the "Apostle to the Heretics.")

The exposed ambiguity between divinity and humanity was not completely resolved even when the Gnostic influence was thought to be vanquished. Gnostic insistence that *the* Logos was purely a spiritual idea of goodness or kindness (*chrestos*) was not sufficient to parry the challenge of John 14:7: "If you knew me, you would know my Father too," and by the fourth century, *Logos* or *chrestos* did become fused with *christos*. How may the product of a collision between a theosophical mythology (insisting on an *apparent* manifestation) and the popular mythological descendant of the old Tammuz-Adonis cult (involving unification of man and the divine being) be explained? (The response has its application to the twentieth as well as to the third century.)

Historicization—the specification of how and when Jesus lived—brought a closure to the controversy between the two distinct streams of a developing edifice: Gnostic *or* Sacrificial, a purely spiritual conception *or* a suffering servant. The evidence in favor of the sacrificial stream was easier to collect and present, the spiritual by definition being nonobservable, existing only as conception. Thus, it seems likely that Docetism was but the recalcitrant reaction to the personification of Logos, the denial that an idea could become a physical existent. Historicization was, then, a *method* of resolving theological dispute; and here it is imperative that an impulse toward anachronization be restrained. *Second-century* historicization involved anthropomorphic application; mythological structures of thought required a corporeal existent. Such structures included the following.

To counter the denial of the body and of sufferings, the virgin-birth doctrine was introduced (reputedly by the incarnationists, Ignatius and John). (It is of some significance that this doctrine, which was to become attached to the origination of a Jesus, was unknown to Paul.) While divine *intervention* in the birth of such biblical characters as Isaac, Joseph, Samson, Samuel, Hezekiah, and Cyrus was part of Judaic tradition, the virgin-birth doctrine revived an even older tradition of divine *impregnation,* which theory succeeded an even more archaic one, that all births were marvellous, being part of the mystery of the female principle. In addition to a divinity feature, biological connection was established through earthly parents; ostensibly, this was to ground a claim to messiahship since the lineage of both parents—with some obvious discrepancies (e.g., the father of Joseph)—was traced back to the House of David. The virgin-birth doctrine was, of course, the vehicle of incarnation and, as Irenaeus (130–200 C.E.), Bishop of Lyons, viewed it, an incarnation was a participation in God, enabling men to become gods.[10]

Another existing structure employed to counter the Doc[k]etic "phantom" was the dispatching of the material body through crucifixion. This required connection to a historical person (Pontius Pilate) representing "official" imperial power to destroy the earthly manifestation of an embodied savior. In a final thrust at the Docetic abstention from the eucharist (because it was not flesh), there was the incorporation of the widespread mythological structure of theophagy, the sacramental eating of the body as a defense against the forces of sin and evil. (See chapter 6 of *The Gospel According to John;* see also the Epistle of Ignatius to the Romans VII, in Lake, *The Apostolic Fathers,* p. 235.)

Thus was concretization and objectification expressed within the earthly presence of a savior-god sacrificed for redemption of humanity. *Objec-*

tification constituted historicity in the second century—so thought the materialists (incarnationists). By the end of the century, the ultimate victory over the spiritualists from within the movement was assured; Docetism was branded a heresy even while the new orthodoxy had absorbed Gnostic thought, i.e., the Logos as being eternal, and a fusion of *Logos, chrestos,* and *christos.* If one needed evidence that the Christian edifice was the result of a diversity of influences and did not emerge from a single source or individual, Gnostic teachings serve as a reminder of its origins and indebtedness.

In contrast to the "historical" features of incarnation, crucifixion, and sacramental communion, one notes the silence of Paul concerning the human career of Jesus. Indeed, two distinct emphases are apparent within the early formative period of development: an obscure central figure versus a prominent one, or a divine career distinguishable from a human career. Paul was not in a position to attest to a connection between a historical Prefect of Judaea named Pilate and a Jesus; he could only aver that the death of Jesus was a result of "evil forces"—hint of a Gnostic characterization. To a new orthodoxy, Paul's first-century silence on the details of a human life of Jesus may even have suggested his belief in a spectral Jesus. For Paul, the figure of Jesus' earthly existence was obscure; his triumph was his rising.

Paul. Paul is probably the best exemplar of kerygmatic certainty; to understand Paul is to comprehend kerygma. His claim to apostolic authority is as a witness to resurrection, set forth in his letters to the Galatians and Corinthians: "I must make it clear to you, my friends, that the gospel you heard me preach is not of human origin. I did not take it over from any one; no one taught it me; I received it through a revelation of Jesus Christ" (Galatians 1:11,12). The theophany to which he refers bears some resemblance to the scene at the Burning Bush of Sinai. What was this gospel received through revelation? "For the love of Christ controls us once we have reached the conclusion that one man died for all and therefore all mankind has died" (2 Corinthians 5:14).[11] It can be seen here that Paul is absolutely unconcerned with a historical setting, since for him, a cosmic event has brought history to an *end:* "God has made the wisdom of the world look foolish!" (1 Corinthians 1:20). An eschatological end-of-time message dominates Paul's thought, and that message can only be apprehended in chiliastic conviction, that is, a sudden happening: The teaching is proclaimed, not at Bethlehem or Nazareth, or even at Golgotha, but at Easter! With the death of Jesus came the death of Death! "What I mean, my friends, is this: Flesh and blood can never possess the kingdom of God, the perishable cannot possess the imperishable. . . . This perishable body must be clothed with the imperishable, and what is mortal with immortality. . . . Death is swallowed up; victory is won!" (*The First Letter of Paul to the Corinthians* 15:50–54).

This chiliastic death of death "in a flash and the twinkling of an eye," as expressed in 1 Corinthians 15:52, brings about the possibility of a new form of existence. (The consequence of Paul's eschatological idea of sacramental participation in the death of a deity could serve as the mystical basis for the existing cult practices of baptism and eucharist.) It is an astounding assertion. For Paul, the death is more significant than the life!

Because of the brilliance of his theological speculation, the quality of genius has been ascribed to Paul as the architect of the Christian cathedral. Yet, what may be overlooked is his political sagacity and shrewdness. Plato's belief in eternal Forms or Ideas solved the problem of mortality (for Plato), probably the most disturbing of all human anxieties; i.e., by sharing in eternal ideas, the soul can survive death and partake of immortality. Paul was politically more astute in going much farther than Plato in his reach. Platonic reasoning about the imperishability of Forms is entirely a product of rational thought. Furthermore, immortality of the spirit is not what humans really desire; such a rationally derived conclusion does not conquer apprehensions and anxieties concerning the death of the body. Only a divine intervention will do—and an astounding miracle at that: Bodily resurrection! In death, a new birth springs forth. Death is *not* triumphant. To share in *that* victory over the grave is worth dying for!

The Bridge Between Heaven and Earth

Underneath the variety of forms of iconic expression lies an idea born at the dawning of human consciousness: an interplay between heaven and earth, the one reflecting the other or influencing the other. In what has been classified as apotropaic art, one finds the pictorial representation of petitionary prayer, the archaic version of "thy will be done on earth, as it is in heaven." Those who drew pictures on a cave wall indicating a successful hunt for food were invoking the power in the cosmos to assist them. Similarly, some of their constructions on earth were designed to influence events in the cosmos; the relationship betrween *there* and *here* was thereby effected. This perceived relationship received a variety of expressions and underwent changes in form throughout eons of time, but there was hardly any doubt that what was done *here* would be of consequence *there*.

In 2 Kings 23:11, one may read of the destruction by a reformer-king of the sun-chariots that had been employed in the Jerusalem Temple courtyard to assist the sun-god in his journey across the sky. Similarly, the lighting of bonfires and tapers on earth at the winter solstice on December 25 would help restore energy to the sun-god so that he could again rise higher in the sky. In another cultural form, the hearts of specially consecrated human victims were physically removed from their cavities and presented to him as sources of courage. One recognizes in these far-distant illustrations the attempt to express the connections between *there* and *here* through the utilization of a magical force held to be operative throughout the universe. A later age related the tale of a legendary king (Arthur) who believed that if he drank from a sacred relic (the chalice used at the Last Supper), it would alleviate drought in his realm, whence the romance of the knightly quest for the Holy Grail. The brisk trade for even a splinter of the wood from the *true* cross, upon which a redeemer was said to have been sacrificed for humanity's sake, stirred the imagination of generations who were convinced that therapeutic qualities were contained in the wood, even as it encouraged not a little deceit on the part of wily and resourceful entrepreneurs. It is not too difficult to recognize that mythical structures were the products of human need and yearnings giving rise to numerological formulae (the lucky and unlucky numbers and days that remain with us), a vast collection of portentous dreams, signs, omens, oracles, and perceived messages or representations from *there* to *here*. Even purely ceremonial expressions—"may you live a long life," "may all your dreams come true"— were regarded as efficacious because *uttered*. While alone not sufficient to command heavenly forces to be cooperative, like the petitions of apotropaic art, utterance was considered liturgically necessary to reassure that the bond between *there* and *here* was operative.

Thus, basic structures of thought were rarely discarded or radically changed; only the forms of expression underwent alteration. If a god (like the sun) could become tired and require an infusion of energy, so could he die and just as surely be born. The human record contains a large catalogue of such deities, as the yearnings of mankind came to be expressed in iconization: sculptured or pictorial, almost always anthropomorphized, that is, representations that reflected human appearance and human behavior. Processes of iconization were developed and refined to produce entities of visible materiality and specialized function: the hunt, the forge, war, agriculture, medicine. (Names were commonly associated with such functions: Diana, Vulcan, Mars, Demeter.) With the development of philosophical and theoretical schools came abstraction of the *principle* of iconization, resulting in poetic expression and speculative portraiture: deities began to have spiritualized functions as creators of peace and love and as authors of salvation and redemption. Much like the architects and builders who worked with stone and granite, the "word builders" were able to "construct an edifice" of a conceptual structure that could induce reverence; purity and wisdom came to be represented or were hypostatized. In anthropomorphic adaptation of the *hope* for salvation, a "Jesus Idea" was crafted and molded from a conceptual model conceived in the creative and poetic imagination, an embodiment of purity and sinlessness, as it exists in heaven, and its projection onto the earth. *Here* and *there* were united.

Some confusions can and do arise from failure to discern anthropomorphization and the "painting" of portraits of purity and salvation or their hypostatization; that is, there is a mistaking of art for empirical substance. How does one know that it is only art? When absolute purity is personified within a human form, without argument or explanation, there is no appreciable difference between this and iconic representation. To say—as does an outstanding scholar—that ". . . [N]o objective and enlightened student of the Gospels can help but be struck by the incomparable superiority of Jesus [as compared with the teachings of other charismatics (in Galilee)]"[12] is an implicit ascription of historiography to these writings, as it is a failure to discern how perfectible craft and sculpture can be. What makes for superiority in the teachings is their total divorcement from place and time; as such, they are nonhistorical art objects. One cannot really make contact with them for they are distant and beyond the reach of ordinary life. They are part of the iconic representation that would bridge heaven and earth. It receives its ultimate *physical* expression in the doctrine of incarnation, not in that of the spiritualized conception of Gnostics.

To retrace momentarily, for Philo, Logos was the intelligible world, the actual ideas and powers of God, unrelated to time and place. In the conception of John, Logos was an *event* expressed in incarnation within a body, an event occurring in a specific time and place that was crucial for mankind. That embodiment was necessary as the immanent aspect of God, his transcendent aspect being much too distant for the conceptualizing capability of humans. For, how does one make contact with a superterrestrial being, a remote deity who is entirely pure and incorruptible?

That problem occupied the best minds in the culture center of Alexandria in the third century C.E., one of whom was the Christian Platonist, Origen (185–255 C.E.). (Some have held Origen to be in the same league of theological creativity as Augustine and Aquinas; for instance, Erasmus was reputed to have remarked that one page of Origen was worth ten of Augustine.) How could a relationship be established between the Creator and his creation? For even though God is utterly One and transcendent, that is, inaccessible, the world of existents is nonetheless overpoweringly present, so there just has to be a bridge between there and here. For Origen, then, the answer was a matter of *logical* necessity; there *had* to be a mediator or intermediary between God and humanity. Thus, creativity of the human mind came into full flower: God had established the world through wisdom, which was one of his attributes, it being impossible, of course, to conceive of God without it. Now wisdom, like all of God's glory, *is* in existence since eternity.[13] Through a dynamic, ever-creative process, God makes this attribute of his *manifest,* that is, available, the manifestation—expressed in human glossary—becoming the intermediary. Thus, knowledge of God is a gift, bestowed on the pure individual freely— but requiring the individual's consent. Difficulty commences as one moves from the logical to the empirical, logical necessity not being yet the equivalent of occurrence. Origen seems to have conflated the two. He was prone to see almost everything as allegory, particularly anything connected with scripture. For instance, the trumpets that Joshua (Yoshua) commanded to be blown at Jericho (Yeriho), creating a seismic disturbance, were actually the apostles of Yoshua (Jesus). From such allegorization it is but an easy step to the mystery of a savior in the flesh. Did the manifestation of which Origen speaks take place? Was there an intermediary redeemer who became human, yet was beyond humanity? Surely, there were many founders of cults, some of whom had absolutely no existence apart from mental processes, who contested for the allegiance of a company of followers. Was the manifestation of God simply an icon, the construct of a fertile mind? Or was it revelation, the gift bestowed on individuals who gave their consent to receive the knowledge that described an attribute of God himself? Not many who have addressed the matter could go beyond the confines of logic and argument. Indeed, casuistry, the reconciliation of disparate conceptual constructs, became the dominant mode of resolution of difficulties.

Going from the second century to the twentieth, one observes the same mode in operation, its essential nature not being altered, as may be seen in the following illustrations. The first presents the evidential base for there being only four gospels. It comes from the work of Irenaeus, a post-apostolic church father, Bishop of Lyons (130–200). Irenaeus was held in high esteem by the renowned church historian Eusebius, who relied on him as a prime source of second-century events. In a work entitled *Adversus Haereses* aimed principally at refuting Gnosticism, particularly that of the Marcionite sect, Irenaeus sets forth his reasons in a fine illustration of casuistic method:

> But it is not possible that the Gospels can be either more or fewer in number than they are. For, since there are four zones of the world in which we live, and four principal winds, while the church has been scattered throughout all the world, and the *pillar and ground* [Timothy 3:15] of

the church is the gospel and the spirit of life; it is fitting that she should have four pillars, breathing incorruption on every side, and vivifying men afresh. From this fact [sic], it is evident that the Word, and the Artificer of all, He that sitteth upon the cherubim, and holds together all things, when He was manifested to men, gave us the gospel under four forms but bound together by one Spirit."[14]

The second illustration from the twentieth century involves the actual content of gospel writings. An author asks why unleavened bread and bitter herbs were not mentioned within any of the synoptic Gospels and their accounts of the Last Supper. After all, *The Gospel According to Luke* 22:15–16 has Jesus declaring: "How I have longed to eat this Passover with you before my death!" In addition, in 1 Corinthians 5:7, Jesus is presented as "Christ our Passover Lamb has been sacrificed."[15] Viewing such writings as historiography, it becomes "logical" to infer that the Last Supper was a Passover meal. If it was a Passover meal, why were traditional foods not mentioned, since Jesus was [in fact] a Jew? (The "fact" requires no more than simple asseveration as something self-evident.) Whether or not the Last Supper was a Passover meal has generated much speculation and investigation and has drained reservoirs of ink. The "conclusive" demonstration that it was *not* a Passover meal has been seen as a satisfactory solution to a thorny problem, while creating other casuistic difficulties for the claims in Luke and Corinthians.

The foregoing question is much like the one that troubled Valentinus and Clement of Alexandria: Was the food that Jesus ate corrupted or not? The line of "investigations" from the second to the twentieth centuries is a direct one: Answers reflect the questions that are asked.

To be sure, there are investigations that go beyond self-confirming knowledge and casuistic method. Somehow these do not seem to penetrate much farther than the specialists at whom they are directed. From the pen of an esteemed twentieth-century critical scholar comes the following markedly different style:

With confidence we must ascribe his birth as well as his early years to the little Galilean town of Nazareth. The fact that all the Gospels make reference to it as the town from which he came awakens confidence, for this is precisely the sort of detail which later imaginations would not have conjured up.[16]

Enough has already been said previously about a group of people—netzerenes—whose belief system was objectified, the locality deriving its name from them. Thus, the blithe assertion of "confidence" of the author is based not on geographical or archaeological evidence, but on reworked writings dominated by theological claims, not historical or geographic concerns. It may be noted that Galilean place-names in New Testament writings had no Christians in them until the fourth-century advent of the Byzantines into Palestine. (As *The Gospel According to Matthew* 11:20,23 puts it, Capernaum, Chorazin, and Bethsaida were among the "impenitent towns" that refused even to accept miracles as evidence.) One may wonder why not one gospel was composed in Galilee; after all, the marvels took place primarily in Galilee and there must have been some places that were not impenitent, say, the larger urban centers of Tiberias and Sepphoris. One may also wonder why, in the first three centuries, Antioch in Hellenized Syria—not Galilee—was the center of the Christian movement. Was it because Galilee was considered a provincial backwoods area, a sort of Erehwon? These are, of course, questions that border on the empirical and do not lend themselves to casuistic treatment.

To ascertain the "secret" of success of a historical movement or institution is difficult. Certainly, the appeal of its message (victory over death) had much to do with it as did the extent of the conviction of its exponents and followers. That it speaks in God's name and has sole possession of a revealed truth makes for a powerful argument. However, as is well-known with mass movements of the twentieth century, organization is critical: An effective apparatus is needed to secure positions of influence that can effectuate mass change within the social organism. Beyond message, argument, and the creation of a literature, mechanism is required.

The Sword Is Mightier Than the Pen

The first centuries of the common era were periods of struggle and intense conflict between competing claims to capture the allegiance of mankind within the Roman imperium. Judaism had been subdued by force of imperial arms while Gnosticism had been routed in intense and blackening polemic, as well as by internal doctrinal and creedal adjustments. For example, the charge of hypocrisy was laid at the door of such Gnostic leaders as Valentinus and Marcion by Tertullian, i.e., that they represented themselves as "pure" *souls* while committing "bodily" evils at the same time. Of course, this kind of charge can come home to roost when one is ensconced on a seat of power. (See p. 125.) Despite the victories of the first and second centuries, in the third and fourth centuries it seemed that the devotees of the saviors Attis and Mithra, imported from the Near East, would sweep the field of counterclaimants within the capital of Rome itself. At the same time, the intellectualized polytheism of Hellas with its blend of neo-Platonism and Stoicism, combined with Gnostic sources outside the Christian Church which attracted the educated class, was fighting a rearguard action against what was regarded as an upstart philosophy.[17] By the beginning of the fourth century, a historicized tale transformed to a literary level became triumphant. It vanquished its opponents in a variety of ways, honorable and less than honorable, for piety was more virtuous than honesty. Deceit and forgery were in evidence, it being nothing to alter an event to fit a prophecy or to alter a prophecy to fit an event. Paul's declaration in Romans 3:7 appeared to justify questionable means to attain sacred ends: "Again, if the truth of God is displayed to his greater glory through my falsehood, why should I any longer be condemned as a sinner?" (In a later age, Picasso's remark that "Art is a lie that reveals the "truth" has often been applied to the parable style of teaching characteristic of gospel writings.) Origen of Alexandria voiced his complaint that his detractors and critics had made his writings unrecognizable—this, in his lifetime!

While some might not characterize the deliberate use of anachronism as a falsehood or lie, it certainly beclouds and distorts a record to speak, as *The Gospel According to John* does (9:22 and 12:42), of the banning of messianists from the synagogue as an occurrence taking place in the lifetime of Jesus, to which Jesus addresses himself. (See p. 111.) There was an ousting of schismatics (*Minim*) from a synagogue in the year 95 C.E. through an imprecation on heretics, as there would be an ousting of a vocally dissident or disruptive group from any orthodox institution. (The branding of Docetists as heretics by those insisting on physical incarnation is but a ready example, as was the anathematizing of Arianism after the Council of Nicaea.)

Certainly, one of the least honorable of ways to win the field was the suppression of critical works through book burning and censorship, the sure indicators of mortal combat and fanatical zeal. In the second century, the *True Doctrine* of Celsus appeared (ca. 178 C.E.), in which there was sharp criticism of Christian doctrines. For example, Celsus charged that the gospels were rewritten several times until the text was fully shaped to the purpose of the writers. He also asked why no punishment was meted out to the judge of Jesus, i.e., Pontius Pilate, whereas one who had disrespected the worship of the god Dionysus was punished severely.[18] This polemic was destroyed upon Christian accession to political power. However, since Origen had replied to Celsus some seventy years later, his refutations had preserved many direct quotations from the work of Celsus. And so, the *True Doctrine* came to be reconstructed from Origen's reply (*Contra Celsum*) in a later, more tolerant era. The same mistake was not repeated a century later when it came to the qualitatively superior works of the polemicist Porphyry criticizing the errors of Christian doctrine. As a careful scholar and chronographer, Porphyry had demonstrated that the Book of Daniel was a work in apocalyptic style (11:21–34) not of the sixth century B.C.E., but of the second century, ca. 175 B.C.E. It became the model for pseudepigraphic, apocalyptic, and deliberately obscure writings, with its content of the successive collapse of imperial powers (ranging from Nebuchadnezzar, Belshazzar, Cyrus, Darius, forth and back) yielding to a universal God-ruled kingdom to be established by an anointed one (*meshiah*). Even though such chronographic work undermined one of the main foundational supports, a *prophecy,* of what was to become Christianity, it was Porphyry's fifteen books *Against the Christians* that was systematically hunted down and destroyed. One can understand why. Porphyry regarded gospel writers as inventors of, not narrators of, events. More methodical was the hunt-down for critical rejoinders to Porphyry, to prevent his poison from being diffused into the body of believers; after all, Origen had kept Celsus alive simply by his rejoinder. The net result of this effort at obliteration was that only fragmentary quotations from Porphyry remain. Harnack considered this work "the most ample and thoroughgoing treatise which has ever been written against Christianity."[19]

It seems rather remarkable that even before its complete realization as a political power, the movement of Christianity was sufficiently well-organized as to be able to exercise effective censorship against would-be critics. As testimony to internal cohesion in the face of sectarian waywardness, *that* may account for its attainment of power. The silencing of opposition was one aspect of disciplined organization; a cadre of creative writers was another. Ultimately, it was, of course, the capture of supreme political power that was decisive, or as Mommsen remarked: "Christianity merely expressed in the religious field what had already been accomplished in the political." The imperialism of Rome became the Christian imperium in 313 C.E. The seat of government would not only beat down any would-be rivals or critics, but it solidified and centralized the new belief system into an absolutism. Following the famed Council of Nicaea in 325, in a letter to the bishops and people, the Emperor Constantine anathematized followers of Bishop Arius as "Porphyrians," and decreed the destruction of Arian works.[20]

In exultant triumph, the sanctioned belief system could now write an officially authorized version of history that it became blasphemous to challenge. Harnack expressed it well:

> We have no information regarding the effect produced by the work [of Porphyry], beyond what may be gathered from the horror displayed by the fathers of the Church. Yet even a literary work of superior excellence

could hardly have won the day. The religion of the Church had become a world religion by the time that Porphyry wrote, and no professor can wage war successfully against such religions, unless his hand grasps the sword of the reformer as well as the author's pen.[21]

The pen, too, was seen as extension of the sword. In a twentieth-century work, an editor has observed: "What is written, they say, remains. From its earliest beginnings, the religion of the Word who himself wrote no word (except one, with His finger, in the dust) was expressed in a literature."[22] Indeed, it was voluminously expressed, quite clearly on the assumption that as long as it is written, it must be so. The belief seems to abide with humanity that what is recorded is historiographic; it could not be otherwise than as stated. Besides, a book of Scripture was absolutely necessary. Mystery religions and civic religions of the State had nothing like the Jewish Scriptures (the Septuagint). The organization had work to do to produce a new edition. The literature that was put forth as the product of the Word consisted of a confession of what was believed, in the form of narratives, apologetics, polemics, episodes, letters, and memoranda encased in a history of the unification of an institution come to be called the Church. This was an ecclesiastical authority that formed the Library of Documents, the dispenser of sanctified rewards (and punishments), joined to a political power center. Thus, a collection of writings around a central theme was assembled and given official imprimatur. It may be observed that the largest mass of collected writings occurred in the second century (not the first), and was directed to communities outside the country of Palestine.

As has already been suggested, one of the features of the collected literature was frankly polemical. The besmirching of opponents and older traditions accompanied a policy of courting the favorable opinion of the imperial government even amid periods of persecution or, perhaps, because of it. Some of the apologetic writings of the second and third centuries are flavored with political protestations as much as they reflect theological argument in an obvious bid for acceptance. For instance, Justin in his *First Apology,* which is addressed to the Emperor Antoninus Pius (138–161 C.E.), assures him that Christians were not participants in the final desperate revolt of Judaea against Roman rule in 131–135 C.E. under the "messiah" Bar Kokhba. As evidence of loyalty to the imperial ruler, he accuses Bar Kokhba of persecution of the Christians because of their devotion to Jesus and their belief in a transnational doctrine.[23] Bar Kokhba's policies have to be seen within the context of a war of desperation against an approaching national extinction. How was one to deal with those like Justin, born in Samaria, who refuse to support the restoration of national honor? Were they subversives against whom military measures were necessary? If not outright traitors, they were Roman partisans who apparently preferred foreign domination to freedom and sovereignty. If one recollects that American Tories were often tarred and feathered by Yankee Doodles zealous for "liberty or death," one can begin to understand the antagonism of the party of Bar Kokhba to Justin's obsequiousness and to his expressed glee over the political downfall of Judaea ("that your land may be desolate and your cities burned with fire"). Justin was an adept at preachment about the removal of "spiritual leaven" and the "circumcision of the heart" (of envy and hatred) even as he exhibited and expressed contumely and hatred.[24] Moreover, since Jews looked askance at the ascription of divinity to a mortal being, it seemed *logical* for a Justin to assign blame to them for deicide.

In Justin's *Dialogue with Trypho* (ca. 160 C.E.) can be seen the twin operations of besmirching and sycophancy, the courting of favor with the ruling power. In a seemingly innocuous expression in chapter 85, Justin declares:

> Every demon is vanquished and subdued when exorcised in the name of this true Son of God who was the First-born of all creatures, who was born of a virgin, who suffered and was crucified by your people under Pontius Pilate. . . .[25]

The term "under" is an alteration of the famous Tacitus "testimony": ". . . had undergone the death penalty . . . by sentence of the procurator Pontius Pilate" (Tacitus, Book XLIV). This single substitution [Justin repeats the phraseology elsewhere]—"under" for "by"—not only appeared to exculpate Roman administration from a judgment of guilt in Christian eyes, but it came to affect the text of the Roman Catholic Mass (*sub Pontio Pilato*) while inspiring and spreading centuries of calumny. The assertion is all the more grievous since *the* crucifixion is here fixed as historical fact; it cannot be left open to allegorical interpretation, e.g., Paul's "evil forces" or a Gnostic-type *apparent* event. The notion of deicide would not make sense, of course, unless God is *not* a psychic phenomenon, but has assumed mortal shape and form. It offered a double-edged proof that the "Word became flesh" inasmuch as the flesh was destructible, and the destroyers can be named and marked with certainty.

Here we see an expression of diabolization, an extension of the feature of aspersing one's theological opponents, which seemed to be a characteristic of the literature collection of 100 to 400 C.E. In addition, the element of theodicy is increasingly apparent. For instance, the "old" testament is the story of a wicked people, and the destruction of their holy city is deserved punishment by God. The "new" testament is spotless, and all who confess its truth participate in spotlessness.

Acrimony is not the intent here; description is. The fall of Jerusalem in 70 C.E. marked the beginning of the Christian era in a very real sense. With the overthrow of the Temple hierarchy, a new hierarchy was to claim divine sanction and authority.[26] Now, part of the Jewish inheritance included a number of variegated sects and organized "heresies against Judaism."(Hegesippus makes mention of these.[27]) Thus, a grand theory of supersession and theodicy was about to be forged, a creative enterprise that would take many years to complete. Supersession is not *mere* replacement or the filling of an empty place. It involves a theodicy of "rightful displacement," a mystical ascent. In Bishop Ignatius's adapation and exegesis of 1 Corinthians 5:7–8, he declares:

> Put aside then the evil leaven, which has grown old and sour, and turn to the new leaven, which is Jesus Christ. . . . For Christianity did not base its faith on Judaism, but Judaism on Christianity. . . .[28]

One can find in the reinterpretation of the Old Testament references to prefiguring (e.g., the stories of Abel and Isaac), foreshadowing, and fulfillment of prophecies. With this idea as a theological base came invidious contrasts: "It has been said to you, but now I say . . ."; the *old* versus the *new* dispensation is probably the best summary. The pen—later to be combined with the sword—produced an exhibition of triumphalism: "See, you are in ruins (as you deserve), while we are exalted." The arrogance of such unkind gloating was ill-suited to an ostensible doctrine of love of enemies, but it was also understandable as a demonstration of ongoing human weakness that could not be "changed in the twinkling of an eye."

Even this was not the ultimate expression of supersessionism. That came in a millennial-long display of supercilious superiority: the painting of a picture of ethical perfection in contrast with an admitted history of imperfection. Origen characterized it as the "spiritual Israel" versus the "carnal Israel." Two examples are offered from the works of outstanding scholars that reveal the effects of centuries of such teachings and tacit understandings. The first is from the pen of F. H. Colson, the learned translator of the works of Philo of Alexandria issued by the Loeb Classical Library of the Harvard University Press.

The author comments that Philo's *Flaccus* might have been left unwritten because of Philo's remarks about divine punishment of Flaccus. Flaccus was Prefect of Alexandria and Egypt in the period of 32 to 41 C.E., during the imperial reign of Tiberius and Gaius (Caligula). The latter had him condemned to exile and subsequent execution. In his introduction, Colson has this to say:

In S[ection] 117 [Editor's error: S 121], the Jews are represented as saying "We do not rejoice at the punishment of an enemy because we have been taught by the Holy Laws to have human sympathy." This is easily said but not so easily done, and if Philo believed that he himself had learnt this lesson, I think he deceived himself. He gloats over the misery of Flaccus in his fall, exile, and death, with a vindictiveness which I feel to be repulsive.[29]

The recounting of the heinous crimes of Flaccus, from releasing mobs and encouraging riots to mass crucifixion spectacles, amid flute-playing, dances, and mimes, does not appear to arouse the translator's repulsion; only the apparent moral inadequacy of Philo does. One wonders whether Colson would have been repulsed by the commentaries on the destruction of Jerusalem in 70 C.E. and the vindictiveness that can be found in some triumphalist fourth-century writings. The following is a comment by eighteenth-century mathematician William Whiston, translator of the complete works of Josephus. Whiston was the successor to the chair in mathematics at Cambridge University previously held by Sir Isaac Newton. The context of the comment is the recounting of the daily crucifixions of prisoners and escapees during the siege of Jerusalem, deliberately designed to break the spirit of the defenders. The translator has this to say in his note: "Reland notices how justly this judgment came upon the Jews since they had brought it on themselves by the crucifixion of their Messiah."[30] The Colson remarks reveal the superciliousness of a legacy of ethical supersessionism while Whiston's reveal the legacy of a vindictive theodicy.[31]

The preachments of learned scholars ring hollow: unfortunately a god of vindictiveness was not replaced by a god of love. There is little reason to admire a *claim* to ethical superiority whether ecclesiastical, political, social, or individual—judging by the fruit it has borne since 313 C.E. There has only been an *announcement* of ethical preeminence, not a demonstration.

"But You Have Believed This Foolish Rumor and You Have Invented for Yourselves a Christ"[32]

It is necessary first to recall Plato. The concept of sinlessness expresses the idea of a universal or Form. Sinfulness is seen in the particular, namely, in the story of the Jewish nation as portrayed in the Old Testament, a nationalism which must perish because of its particularity, as all particulars must perish. However, sinlessness as a universal, a perfect Form, is immortal. So powerful is this pictorial image that one does not ask whether sinlessness can enter the world as a *Being,* in the flesh. Plato taught that universals were eternal, and the incarnation was but a demonstration of that principle.

In the debate between Trypho and Justin, Justin, of course, refutes all of Trypho's counterarguments, the outcome of such dialogues never really being in doubt. But the charge of a "foolish rumor" (part of a well-known Greek saying) raised in the second century probes deeply: did a personal redeemer die for me? If I affirm the identification of He=Me, do I, thereby, participate in everlasting life? Carried to its ultimate expression, would a martyr's death imitate the ultimate sacrifice? Indeed, the act was sometimes *deliberately* sought out in order to bear witness (one meaning of the term martyr acutally being "witness") and as a means of identification with the master's life. As Bishop Ignatius said: "Suffer me to follow the example of the passion of my God."[33]

In following Bultmann's call for demythologizing, depersonifying would abandon the illusion of a historical figure, the relationship to historical events being more of an unnecessary baggage train. Now, a Christianity without a historical Jesus would be too much for some to take; in fact, it would be a contradiction. A ready and reflexive response would likely inquire: How could gospel narratives have been composed? Legendary details is one thing, fiction another; there just *has to be* a nucleus of fact. When dealing with an *idée fixe,* repetition is necessary: the reflexive response is pure cultural prepossession and tendentious argument, the individuals believing what they are already predisposed to accept. "How could such a story be invented or constructed?" is not a question; it is a "self-evident" answer. As Albert Schweitzer remarked:" Often what is self-evident is least evident." The nucleus of fact may be located in the existing materials, e.g., self-sacrifice, forgiveness of enemies, charitableness —qualities that are available upon exercise; they do not require objectification or iconization. Yet, human creativity synthesizes such qualities within the figure of an idealized human being. As long as there is awareness of the idealization, no difficulty ensues, i.e., if *that* were the nucleus of fact, not much controversy would take place. However, to proclaim "not Jesus as a historical *figure* (since he is beyond recapture anyway) but Christ as a historical *force*" is simply word exchange and amounts to the same idea: it proclaims that there is a reality outside history, that there was a divine intervention and eschatological event occurring in the first century —the overcoming of death itself. It expresses what William James characterized as the "will to believe" and represents a rear-guard action: kerygma, as a last retort, namely, that there *is* a force outside history more powerful than death.

In referring to Paul's experience on the road to Damascus in which he is temporarily blinded by a heavenly vision, author Max I. Dimont speaks of it as a "reality which creates history."[34] He is quick to make clear that he does not intend to convey the idea that a divine drama took place. Instead, the phrase is intended to indicate that reports garbed in the authority of antiquity—however distorted they may be—if advanced by a cadre of believers will *make* history. In fact, an authoritative fabricated "truth" will persist in indestructibility to the point where there occurs a presumption of truth even by nonbelievers. Now, if the "reality" that is advanced happens to be that a divine force has itself entered the historical arena, whether or not it is true is not the critical point. What is critical is whether or not it is believed. One would be hard-pressed to find support among academic historians for such a view in connection with the convulsions of World War I or World War II, or even in the Holy Crusades at the end of the eleventh century. Despite the battle cry "God Wills It," was a force outside history operative in this venture? Even Bultmann recognized that individuals in the twentieth century typically do not behave *as if* they harbored any thought that history had been permanently altered at some point in the first century by a victory over death.

While resolution of the question eludes us, it is, of course, evident that a millennial legacy of conviction has produced outstanding cultural monuments such as magnificent cathedrals and art creations that express the burning faith of their creators. All too often, however, a monument is confused with a fact. For example, Bach's *Mass in B Minor* and the *St. Matthew Passion* are fabulous creations and testimonies of what the Jesus idea meant to the composer. Much as these works are to be admired and treasured for their inspirational quality and as exemplars of the heights to which human accomplishment can extend, they cannot be mistaken for evidence of the tomb of Jesus or for the veracity of the crucifixion story as empirical occurrence. Similarly, the monument that Constantine ordered to be constructed, subsequently to be known as the Church of the Holy Sepulcher, was a memorial to the depth of his conviction, but that, by itself, did not guarantee the authenticity of the site or the historicity of the person. That poetry, music, and the art of the architect are testimonies of conviction and faith, as well as demonstrations of the powers inhering in the human mind, goes without saying. They are not and cannot be offered as evidence of a historical event as commonly understood.

Does an abandonment of the illusion of a historical figure imply the abandonment of hope? It has been argued that The Jesus Idea was, from the start, an expression of hope for salvation (*yeshua*), but it is necessary to refine the concept of salvation. If it is conceived as victory over death, the first-century dream of Paul that found a ready response to his appeal now would ring hollow even with a fond "will to believe." If salvation is conceived as a state of grace and as release from a sinful nature through identification with a sinless sacrifice, the effective result has been to encourage moral passivity, if not to anesthetize human will. Individuals do not have to do much; they could rest secure in the thought that there *was* a perfect *salvator* who effected their release from sinfulness. For, what else does it mean to say "Lamb of God who takes away the sins of the world"? What need one do more than declare "Amen"?

There is a species of spiritualized pragmatism that insists on the reality of a historical figure. It offers as proof an argument based on what it perceives to be the consequences of lasting impact of belief in a Christ. Origen, for instance, thought that no other leader in human history— emperor, general, philosopher—had a greater effect on human life than the figure of Jesus.[35] Like Moses, Jesus was a historical person *because* he transmitted moral energy to human beings in the present. That energy was expressed in meekness and tranquility, love of mankind, kindness, and gentleness sufficient to convert people from evil-doing. Thus, the whole world had evidence of Jesus' existence and his continual moral reformation of mankind. Given the gnosticism of Origen's spirituality and his tendency to spiritualize all materiality onto a mystical ladder extending heavenwards, he offers a profound and earnest prayer, a picture of the beautiful "reality" in moral reformation. Needless to say, he projects the picture that he paints on to externality as fact.

Another expression of an argument from consequences was presented in these words: ". . . the sheer weight of Christian character carried off allegories and myths, bore down the school of Celsus and the more powerful school of Plutarch, Porphyry, and Plotinus, and abolished the ancient world, and then captured and transformed the Northern nations."[36] Celsus and Porphyry and the ancient world-views they represented were, of course, destroyed by the zeal of singleminded censors. The author mistakes political supremacy, the capture of an imperium, for the demonstration of superiority in character.

Even the substitution of a purely practical argument, rather than a religious conceptualization, offers little change. The moral value of the teachings of Jesus is needed to preserve us from anarchy; thus, the consequences of the belief are a test of its veracity. Such a view rests on an assumption of the moral vacuity of mankind at large, requiring a supernormal exhibition of moral perfection that can be admired from a distance, much as one admires the work of a fine artist, his sculpture or painting. Appreciation and admiration are not yet the same as performance in an art form, nor are they expected to be. In fine-art expression and display, an audience or auditor is necessary, the producer requiring the consumer of the product. In moral behavior, an auditor, i.e., one who does not perform, is amoral. Thus, the effect of the view that a paragon of virtue is necessary to restrain mankind from moral anarchy induces instead the selfsame passivity as the religious belief, which could point to an image or picture of perfection as the possessor of all virtue, even as it cultivated a dangerous illusion: In *Him,* I too am virtuous and sinless. To be sure, there are unusual individuals (e.g., Francis of Assisi, Albert Schweitzer) who took it upon themselves to fashion their behavior in the image of an esteemed ideal into which they breathed the breath of life.

Salvation Refined

In rejecting Gnosticism in the second and third centuries, "materialists" insisted that a phantom spirit of salvation, or The Jesus Idea, was insufficient. What was needed was a real embodiment of the divine so that it could be *seen.* From an abstraction—a Logos—came a human embodiment, *The* Logos, not far off, but here. Yet, that very embodiment or fulfillment has produced another abstraction, transcendent morality. For the danger inherent in creating an unsullied portrait of sinlessness as the repository of absolute virtue is its relocation; it now resides in heaven, far removed and ineffable. I can only *talk* about its inaccessible and untouchable beauty. Thus, it does not matter whether or not I ingest divine qualities in a physical act or in a spiritual expression of symbolic identification, the effect is the same: a divide between self and obligation. In Him, I *am* virtuous, in Him, I *am* sinless; without Him, I am without grace. A gnostic heresy returns to plague the faithful, a phantom disembodied spirit detached from the lives of ordinary humans. What is needed is the exchange of "a foolish rumor" for a refined concept of salvation, i.e., that it does not inhere in a confession of belief at all. As one is able to prepare and dress a scapegoat for sacrifice, so one is able to adorn and adore an appointed surrogate, to represent the discharge of ethical obligations. Regrettably, appointing another, or pointing *to* another, are historically tried—and institutionally sanctified—methods of avoidance. Human redemption is possible only with the recognition that the preachment of virtue is a vain thing, an actual impediment to its realization. Only its demonstration matters.

Notes

The Characteristics of a Good Story

1. John Anderson, "Unveiling a Wilde Salome," *Newsday,* 21 June 1991, p. 21.

The Misconstrual of Allegory

2. C. H. Oldfather (trans.), *The Library of History of Diodorus of Sicily,* vol. 2, book 4, 9:1–10 (Cambridge: Harvard University Press, 1946), pp. 369–73.

The Idea of Idea

3. "The Wisdom of Sirach," 6:22–28, *The Apocrypha,* trans. Edgar J. Goodspeed (New York: Random House Inc., 1959), pp. 234–35.

4. Ibid., 24:19–22, p. 269.

5. Ibid., "The Wisdom of Solomon" 18:14–16, p. 216.

6. Ibid., 7:24–25; 8:17, pp. 191, 193.

7. Robert M. Grant, *Gnosticism and Early Christianity* (New York: Columbia University Press, 1966), pp. 7, 8.

8. Gnostic sect names were derived from leaders such as Cerinthus, Valentinus, Marcion, and Basilides. Others were named after a place of origin or their doctrines (as in Docetism) or their activities (Encratites, "continent ones"). Names were probably assigned by opponents and illustrate the variety of sects within Gnosticism.

Grant, p. 6, referring to Clement of Alexandria's *Stromateis* VII 108. 1–2.

9. Certainly, casuistic questions could easily arise from such teaching and did; for instance, the corruptibility of the food that Jesus ate, i.e., how his divinity could be manifested in this most physical of physical acts.

Clement of Alexandria (150–214 C.E.) cites an excerpt from a letter of the Gnostic, Valentinus: "He [Jesus] ate and drank in a manner peculiar to himself and the food did not pass out of his body. Such was the power of his continence that food was not corrupted within him; for he himself was not subject to the process of corruption" (*Stromateis,* III 59.3, cited in W. E. G. Floyd, *Clement of Alexandria's Treatment of the Problem of Evil* [London: Oxford University Press, 1971], p. 77).

10. "Unity of God and Man Secured by the Incarnation," cited in *A New Eusebius,* ed. J. Stevenson (London: Holy Trinity Church, 1957), p. 123.

11. The element of *control* from the outside appears as the dominant factor in the kerygmatic certainty of a Luther, Schweitzer, and Bultmann.

The Bridge Between Heaven and Earth

12. Geza Vermes, *Jesus the Jew* (New York: Macmillan Publishing Company, 1973), pp. 223–24.

13. Charles Kannengiesser and William L. Petersen, *Origen of Alexandria: His World and His Legacy* (Notre Dame, Ind.: University of Notre Dame Press, 1988).

14. Irenaeus, *Adversus Haereses* III. 11.8 (ed. W. W. Harvey), "Four Gospels Only," cited in J. Stevenson (ed.), *A New Eusebius* (London: Holy Trinity Church, 1957), p. 122.

Irenaeus's argument was probably part of a concerted effort to limit the versions of gospel writings that were available, as well as to curb further creations.

15. Howard C. Kee, *The Origins of Christianity* (Englewood Cliffs, N.J.: Prentice Hall, 1973), p. 55.

16. Morton S. Enslin, *The Prophet from Nazareth* (New York: McGraw-Hill Book Company, 1961), p. 39.

The Sword Is Mightier Than the Pen

17. Among the neo-Platonists of renown was Porphyry, follower of the philosopher Plotinus, born in Tyre (ca. 232–305 C.E.). Among his many written works was a life of Plotinus, who held that Logos was the mind of God, and that the Ideas or Forms were the products of that mind, i.e., what we call thoughts. In addition, Porphyry authored fifteen books of polemic *Against the Christians,* most of which were destroyed, only fragmentary quotations remaining.

Adolf Harnack, *The Mission and Expansion of Christianity in the First Three Centuries* (New York: Harper Brothers, Harper Torchbooks, 1961), pp. 504ff.

18. Henry Chadwick (trans.), *Origen: Contra Celsum,* II:27 (Cambridge, England: At the University Press, 1965), p. 90.

In II:34 (p. 95), Origen replied that the Jewish people—not a Roman judge—was punished: "This nation has been condemned by God and *torn in pieces,* and scattered all over the earth, a fate more terrible than the rending suffered by Pentheus" (the blasphemer of Dionysus as god).

In the same section, Origen also criticizes Celsus for omitting 27:19 of *The Gospel According to Matthew,* which tells how Pilate's wife—troubled by her dreams—advised her husband not to have anything to do with the matter. (Who could know that the wife of Pontius Pilate did not accompany him to Judaea but had remained in Rome? The detail, of course, spoils a good story by the authors of Matthew and his apologist, Origen.)

Roman law did not permit the wives of provincial administrators to accompany them to official posts (transcribed in the Justinian Code, L.iv.2). According to Suetonius (*The Lives of the Caesars*), some emperors (e.g., Tiberius) were considerate enough to provide concubines for appointees on provincial assignment.

There were only two procurators of Judaea (the title instituted during Claudius's reign, 41–54 C.E.) whose wives were with them. One was Felix, who married a Jewish woman, Drusilla, during his term of office in Judaea, 52–60 C.E. (Josephus, *Antiquities,* XX, vii.2; also, *Acts of the Apostles* 24:24); the second was Gessius Florus (64–66 C.E.) whose wife Cleoptra was an intimate friend of Emperor Nero's wife. In making specific mention that Florus's wife accompanied him to Judaea, Josephus (*Antiquities,* XX, xi.1) underscored an unusual practice.

19. Harnack, p. 504.

20. Eusebius, *Historia Ecclesia,* I. 9:30–31, *Letter of Constantine to the bishops and people,* cited in *A New Eusebius,* ed. J. Stevenson (London: Holy Trinity Church, 1957), p. 384.

21. Harnack, p. 509.

22. *A Treasury of Early Christianity: An Anthology of the Writings of the Church Fathers,* ed. Anne Fremantle (New York: The Viking Press, 1953), p. 1.

23. "Justin: First Apology," in Walter J. Black, *Marcus Aurelius and His Times* (New York: The Classics Club, 1945), p. 279.

24. "Indeed the custom of circumcising the flesh . . . was given to you as a distinguishing mark. . . . The purpose of this was that you and only you might suffer the afflictions that are now justly yours; that only your land be desolate, and your cities ruined by fire . . ." ("Dialogue With Trypho," in *Writings of Saint Justin Martyr,* Fathers of the Church Series, ed. Thomas B. Falls [New York: Christian Heritage Inc., 1948], p. 172.

25. Ibid., p. 283.

The *Letter of Ignatius to the Trallians* IX also employs the phrase "*under* Pilate": "be deaf when anyone speaks to you apart from Jesus Christ . . . who was truly born, both ate and drank, was truly persecuted under Pontius Pilate . . ." (Kirsopp Lake [trans.], *The Apostolic Fathers,* vol. 1, IX [Cambridge: Harvard University Press, 1952], p. 221 and I, p. 253).

It may be seen that the statement is directed against Docetic teachings regarding the phantom nature of Jesus.

The phrase "*under* Pilate" is again found in "Ignatius to the Smyrnaeans."

26. One may note that certain structures and institutions in noticeable decline in the thought and practice of first-century Judea were actually restored by a nascent Christian movement which claimed the legitimacy of succession:

Original	Replacement
The end of the monarchical system, even in its attenuated nominal form since 37 B.C.E.	A hierarchy ruled over by an absolute monarch appointed by God.
Weakened belief and trust in marvels and miracles.	Construction of a theological system based on a collection of marvels and miracles.

| End of the sacrificial system and the priesthood. | The ritual of the Mass, involving divine sacrifice, the priest as performer of the miracle of the sacrifice. |

27. "Now, Hegesippus, in the five treatises that have come down to us, has left us a very complete record of his own opinion. . . . The same author also describes the heresies that once arose among the Jews, saying: 'And there were different opinions among the circumcision, among the children of the Israelites against the tribe of Judas and the Christ. These were: Essenes, Galileans, Hemero-baptists, Masobothei, Samaritans, Sadducees, and Pharisees.' " (*Eusebius Pamphili, Ecclesiastical History,* Book IV, chapter 22, trans. Roy J. Deferrari [New York: Fathers of the Church, Inc., 1953], pp. 253, 255.)

28. "Letter of Ignatius to the Magnesians," *The Apostolic Fathers,* vol. 1, X, trans. Kirsopp Lake (Cambridge: Harvard University Press, 1952), p. 207.

29. *Philo,* vol. 9, "Introduction to *In Flaccum,*" trans. F. H. Colson (Cambridge: Harvard University Press, 1954), p. 301.

30. *Wars of the Jews,* Book V, Chapter 11, "Note," in *Josephus: Complete Works,* trans. William Whiston (Grand Rapids, Mich.: Kregel Publications), 1985, p. 565. Editor Whiston's note in *Josephus* reminds one of *The Gospel According to Luke* 19:27: "But as for those enemies of mine who did not want me for their king, bring them here and slaughter them in my presence."

31. A present-day example of a legacy of supersessionism and invalidation appeared in the program notes of a performance of Bach's *Mass in B Minor.* Referring to the *music* of the *Christe eleison,* the notes read: "The gentle elegance and *affeti amorosi* contrast with the preceding fugue, suggesting the more forgiving New Testament God" (*Program of St. John's Chorale* at the Cathedral of the Incarnation, Garden City, New York, March 29, 1992).

"But You Have Believed This Foolish Rumor and You Have Invented for Yourselves a Christ"

32. *Dialogue with Trypho, writings of Saint Justin Martyr* (The Fathers of the Church Series), ed. Thomas B. Falls (New York: Christian Heritage Inc., 1940), p. 161.

"The charge of Trypho was that Christ was an invention, deified in much the same way as the Emperor Hadrian deified his slave lover Antinous in 137 C.E.: *by proclamation* and by building a city on the Nile River named for him" (Eusebius quoting Hegesippus, *Eusebius: The Ecclesiastical History,* vol. 1, IV: 8, trans. Kirsopp Lake [Cambridge: Harvard University Press, 1953], p. 321).

Trypho may have been a fictitious personality. Dialogues were often written where the opponent was a foil for the presentation of counterarguments by the writer. As represented in this dialogue, Trypho(n) was said to have been a native of Palestine (like Justin). He became a refugee after the failed Bar Kokhba revolt and now resided in one of the Greek city-states of Asia Minor where he and

Justin engaged in debate. The "debate" seems to be a contrivance for a discourse by Justin.

33. "Letter of Ignatius to the Romans," VI, *The Apostolic Fathers,* vol. 1, trans. Kirsopp Lake (Cambridge: Harvard University Press, 1952), p. 235. See also IV, p. 231: "Suffer me to be eaten by the wild beasts through whom I can attain to God. . . . Rather entice the wild beasts that they may become my tomb, and leave no trace of my body. . . . Then shall I be truly a disciple of Jesus Christ, when the world shall not even see my body."

34. Max I. Dimont, *Jews, God, and History* (New York: New American Library of World Literature, Inc., 1964), p. 142.

35. Henry Chadwick (trans.), *Origen: Contra Celsum,* I:30 (Cambridge, England: At the University Press, 1965), pp. 29, 30.

36. T. R. Glover, *The Conflict of Religions in the Early Roman Empire,* 8th ed. (London: Methuen and Co., 1919), p. 261.